**FREE DVD**  **FREE DVD**

CASAC Exam DVD from Trivium Test Prep!

Dear Customer,

Thank you for purchasing from Trivium Test Prep! We're honored to help you prepare for your AP exam.

To show our appreciation, we're offering a **FREE *CASAC Essential Test Tips* DVD by Trivium Test Prep**. Our DVD includes 35 test preparation strategies that will make you successful on the AP Exam. All we ask is that you email us your feedback and describe your experience with our product. Amazing, awful, or just so-so: we want to hear what you have to say!

To receive your **FREE *CASAC Essential Test Tips*** DVD, please email us at 5star@triviumtestprep.com. Include "Free 5 Star" in the subject line and the following information in your email:

1. The title of the product you purchased.

2. Your rating from 1 – 5 (with 5 being the best).

3. Your feedback about the product, including how our materials helped you meet your goals and ways in which we can improve our products.

4. Your full name and shipping address so we can send your **FREE *CASAC Essential Test Tips*** DVD.

If you have any questions or concerns please feel free to contact us directly at 5star@triviumtestprep.com. Thank you!

- **Trivium Test Prep Team**

Contents

Introduction 5

What is the IC&RC Alcohol and Drug Counselor Examination? 5

How is the IC&RC Alcohol and Drug Counselor Examination scored? 5

How is the IC&RC Alcohol and Drug Counselor Examination Administered? 6

What's on the IC&RC Alcohol and Drug Counselor Examination? 6

    Domain 1: Clinical Evaluation 6

    Domain 2: Treatment Planning 7

    Domain 3: Referral 7

    Domain 4: Service Coordination 7

    Domain 5: Counseling 8

    Domain 6: Client, Family, and Community Education 9

    Domain 7: Documentation 9

    Domain 8: Professional and Ethical Responsibilities 10

About Trivium Test Prep 11

How to Use This Guide 11

We Want to Hear from You 11

Knowledge of Alcohol and Substance Abuse 12

    Key Concepts in Addiction and Alcoholism 12

    Drug Administration and Testing 16

    Models of Alcoholism and Addiction 19

    Health and Recovery 25

    Prevention, Intervention, and Treatment Modalities 27

    Experiential Practicums 35

Alcoholism and Substance Abuse Counseling 36

    Health Issues 36

    Skills for the Alcoholism Counselor 40

    Group Skills Exhibited by Counselors 41

    Crisis Intervention and Resolution 41

    Individual Counseling 42

Goal of Individual Counseling 43

Methods of Individual Therapy 43

Vocational Rehabilitation 48

Group Counseling 51

The Attributes of a Group Counselor 51

Counseling for Families, Couples, and Significant Others 53

Experiential Practicums 56

Health Issues 56

Experiential Therapy 56

Family and Addiction 58

Overview of Family and Addiction Issues 58

Domestic Violence 60

Substance Abuse and Adolescents 63

Counseling Adolescents 65

Assessment of Substance Abuse, Lethality, and Level of Care 65

Rehabilitation and Treatment Programs 66

Relapse Prevention 66

Substance Abuse and Pre-Adolescents 67

Experiential Practicum 68

Spirituality, Change and Motivation 69

Spirituality 69

Issues of Spirituality in Recovery 69

Motivational Counseling 71

The Benefits of Motivational Counseling 72

The Phases of Motivational Counseling 72

Experiential Practicums 73

Assessment, Clinical Evaluation, Treatment Planning, Family and Community
Education and Case Management 75

Assessment of Substance Abuse, Lethality, and Levels of Care 75

Six Areas of Assessment 75

How Screening and Assessment Differ 75

Factors that Influence Screening and Assessment 76

Substance Abuse Screening Tools 76

Substance Use Assessment 77

The Assessment Interview 77

The Psychosocial History 78

Assessment Tools for Substance Use Disorders 80

Addiction Counseling – Clinical Screening and Assessment 81

Clinical Screening 81

Clinical Assessment 84

Person-Centered Treatment Planning and Co-Occurring Mental Disorders 87

Co-Occurring Mental Disorders 87

Configuration Styles 88

Case Management Principles and Techniques 89

Primary Treatment and Treatment Planning 92

Stress Management 97

Community-Based Prevention 99

Experiential Practicum 112

Professional Responsibility and Ethics 116

Practice Examination 128

Answers and Explanations 166

Introduction

Congratulations on selecting a career as a Credentialed Alcoholism and Substance Abuse Counselor (CASAC). You are undertaking difficult, rewarding and necessary work, but you will make a difference in the lives of the people whom you help to treat every day.

This guide will provide you with a detailed overview of the IC&RC Alcohol and Drug Counselor Examination for CASAC certification, so you know exactly what to expect on test day. We'll take you through all the concepts covered on the test and give you the opportunity to test your knowledge with practice questions. Even if it's been a while since you last took a major test, don't worry; we'll make sure you're more than ready!

What is the IC&RC Alcohol and Drug Counselor Examination?

The IC&RC Alcohol and Drug Counselor Examination is offered by the International Certification and Reciprocity Consortium (IC&RC). It is based on alcohol and drug counselor job descriptions and analyses. IC&RC contracts with Schroeder Management Technologies to develop and administer, and score the exam through ISO-Quality Testing (IQT). It is one of four requirements for application to the CASAC credentialing unit of the New York State Office of Alcoholism and Substance Abuse Services (OASAS) as part of the credentialing process; candidates must also meet certain requirements in competence and ethical conduct, work experience, and education. Please consult with OASAS for further details on eligibility.

How is the IC&RC Alcohol and Drug Counselor Examination scored?

Official scores become available two to three weeks after the exam and are reported by ISO to IC&RC; however, you will receive your preliminary scores immediately after the computer-based examination. Each multiple-choice question is worth one raw point. The total number of questions you answer correctly is added up to obtain your raw score. Raw scores are scaled from 200 – 800; a passing score is 500. The scaling takes question difficulty into account, so not every question is weighted equally.

There may be some questions on the test that are not scored; however, you will not know which ones these are. ISO uses these to test out new questions for future exams.

How is the IC&RC Alcohol and Drug Counselor Examination Administered?

The exam is required by the New York State Office of Alcoholism and Substance Abuse Services (OASAS) but administered by the IC&RC. It is a computer-based test offered on a continuous basis by ISO Quality Testing in Albany, Binghamton, Buffalo, Flushing (Queens), New York City, and Syracuse. Students may re-take the exam every sixty days. You may cancel or reschedule your exam up to five days prior to test day. You can register for the exam, pay the registration fee, and check exam locations and dates at www.iqttesting.com.

You will need to print your Candidate Admission Letter from your online account and bring it, along with your identification, to the testing site on test day. You may not bring personal items with you into the testing center. No books, papers, or cellphones are allowed.

What's on the IC&RC Alcohol and Drug Counselor Examination?

This test measures the knowledge and skills expected for a Credentialed Alcoholism and Substance Abuse Counselor. The certification examination will test you in eight domains. The learning objectives of each are listed here:

Domain 1: Clinical Evaluation

- Demonstrate effective verbal and non-verbal communication to establish rapport.

- Discuss with the client the rationale, purpose, and procedures associated with the screening and assessment process to facilitate client understanding and cooperation.

- Assess the client's current situation, including signs and symptoms of intoxication and withdrawal, by evaluating observed behavior and other available information to determine client's immediate needs.

- Administer the appropriate screening and assessment instruments specific to the client's age, developmental level, culture, and gender in order to obtain objective data to assess client's current problems and needs.

- Obtain relevant history and related information from the client and other pertinent sources in order to establish eligibility and appropriateness to facilitate the assessment process.

- Screen and assess for physical, medical, and co-occurring disorders that might require additional assessment and referral.

- Interpret data results in order to integrate all available information, formulate diagnostic impressions, and determine appropriate action.

- Summarize assessment results in order to document and support the diagnostic impressions and treatment recommendations.

Domain 2: Treatment Planning

- Discuss diagnostic assessment and recommendations with the client and concerned others to initiate an individualized treatment plan that incorporates client's strengths, needs, abilities, and preferences.

- Formulate and prioritize mutually agreed-upon problems, immediate and long-term goals, measurable objectives, and treatment methods based upon assessment findings for facilitating a course of treatment.

- Use ongoing assessment and collaboration with the client to review and modify the treatment plan to address treatment needs.

Domain 3: Referral

- Identify client needs that cannot be met in the current treatment setting.

- Match client needs with community resources appropriate to their abilities, gender, sexual orientation, developmental level, culture, ethnicity, age, and health status to remove barriers and facilitate positive client outcomes.

- Identify needs differentiating between self-referral and counselor referral.

- Explain to the client the rationale for the referral to facilitate the client's participation with community resources.

- Continually evaluate referral sources to determine effectiveness and outcome of the referral.

Domain 4: Service Coordination

- Identify and maintain information about current community resources in order to meet identified client needs.

- Communicate with community resources concerning relevant client information to meet the identified needs of the client.

- Advocate for the client in areas of identified needs to facilitate continuity of care.

- Evaluate the effectiveness of case management activities through collaboration with the client, treatment team members, and community resources to ensure quality service coordination.

- Consult with the client, family, and concerned others to make appropriate changes to the treatment plan ensuring progress toward treatment goals.

- Prepare accurate and concise screening, intake, and assessment documents.

Domain 5: Counseling

- Develop a therapeutic relationship with clients, families, and concerned others in order to facilitate self-exploration, disclosure, and problem solving.

- Educate the client regarding the structure, expectations, and limitations of the counseling process.

- Utilize individual and group counseling strategies and modalities to match the interventions with the client's level of readiness.

- Continually evaluate the client's level of risk regarding personal safety and relapse potential in order to anticipate and respond to crisis situations.

- Apply selected counseling strategies in order to enhance treatment effectiveness and facilitate progress towards completion of treatment objectives.

- Adapt counseling strategies to match the client's needs including abilities, gender, sexual orientation, developmental level, culture, ethnicity, age, and health status.

- Evaluate the effectiveness of counseling strategies based on the client's progress in order to determine the need to modify treatment strategies and treatment objectives.

- Develop an effective continuum of recovery plan with the client in order to strengthen ongoing recovery outside of primary treatment.

- Assist families and concerned others in understanding substance use and utilizing strategies that sustain recovery and maintain healthy relationships.

- Document counseling activity to record all relevant aspects of treatment.

Domain 6: Client, Family, and Community Education

- Provide culturally relevant formal and informal education that raises awareness of substance use, prevention, and recovery.

- Provide education on issues of cultural identity, ethnic background, age, sexual orientation, and gender in prevention, treatment, and recovery.

- Provide education on health and high-risk behaviors associated with substance use, including transmission and prevention of HIV/AIDS, tuberculosis, sexually transmitted infections, hepatitis, and other infectious diseases.

- Provide education on life skills, including but not limited to, stress management, relaxation, communication, assertiveness, and refusal skills.

- Provide education on the biological, medical, and physical aspects of substance use to develop an understanding of the effects of chemical substances on the body.

- Provide education on the emotional, cognitive, and behavioral aspects of substance use to develop an understanding of the psychological aspects of substance use, abuse, and addiction.

- Provide education on the sociological and environmental effect of substance use to develop an understanding of the impact of substance use on the affected family systems.

- Provide education on the continuum of care and resources available to develop an understanding of prevention, intervention, treatment, and recovery.

Domain 7: Documentation

- Protect client's rights to privacy and confidentiality according to best practices in preparation and handling of records, especially regarding the communication of client information with third parties.

- Obtain written consent to release information from the client and/or legal guardian, according to best practices and administrative rules, to exchange relevant client information with other service providers.

- Document treatment and continuing care plans that are consistent with best practices and applicable administrative rules.

- Document client's progress in relation to treatment goals and objectives.

- Prepare accurate and concise reports and records including recommendations, referrals, case consultations, legal reports, family sessions, and discharge summaries.

- Document all relevant aspects of case management activities to assure continuity of care.

Domain 8: Professional and Ethical Responsibilities

- Adhere to established professional codes of ethics and standards of practice in order to promote the best interests of the client and the profession.

- Adhere to jurisdictionally-specific rules and regulations regarding best practices in substance use disorder treatment in order to protect and promote client rights.

- Recognize individual differences of the counselor and the client by gaining knowledge about personality, cultures, lifestyles, gender, sexual orientation, special needs, and other factors influencing client behavior to provide services that are sensitive to the uniqueness of the individual.

- Continue professional development through education, self-evaluation, clinical supervision, and consultation in order to maintain competence and enhance professional effectiveness.

- Identify and evaluate client issues that are outside of the counselor's scope of practice and refer to other professionals as indicated.

- Advocate for populations affected by substance use and addiction by initiating and maintaining effective relations with professionals, government entities, and communities to promote availability of quality services.

- Apply current counseling and psychoactive substance use research literature to improve client care and enhance professional growth.

About Trivium Test Prep

Trivium Test Prep uses industry professionals with decades' worth of knowledge in their fields, proven with degrees and honors in law, medicine, business, education, the military, and more, to produce high-quality test prep books for students.

Our study guides are specifically designed to increase any student's score, regardless of his or her current skill level. Our books are also shorter and more concise than typical study guides, so you can increase your score while significantly decreasing your study time.

How to Use This Guide

This guide is not meant to waste your time on superfluous information or concepts you've already learned. Because we have eliminated the filler and fluff, you'll be able to work through the guide at a significantly faster pace than you would with other test prep books. By allowing you to focus only on those concepts that will increase your score, we'll make your study time shorter and more effective.

We Want to Hear from You

Here at Trivium Test Prep, our goal is to keep our guides concise, show you a few test tricks along the way, and ultimately help you achieve your goals. We hope that, with the help of this guide, you've learned all the information you needed to pass the exam and have exceeded even your own expectations.

On that note, we're always interested in your feedback. Please email us at feedback@triviumtestprep.com to let us know if we've truly prepared you for the exam. (And feel free to include your test score!)

Your success is our success. Good luck!

Sincerely,

The Trivium Test Prep Team

Some information in this guide is courtesy of The U.S. Department of Health and Human Services, Substance Abuse and Mental Health Services Administration, Technical Assistance Publication Series 21: Addiction Counseling Competencies, *The Knowledge, Skills, and Attitudes of Professional Practice,* March 2006.

Knowledge of Alcohol and Substance Abuse
(85 Hours)

Key Concepts in Addiction and Alcoholism

Addiction is characterized by the inability to stop using or drinking despite negative consequences such as:

- inability to keep a job or attend school
- use of substances in high risk situations, such as while driving
- legal consequences due to use of drugs or alcohol
- encountering conflicts due to alcohol or substance use
- damage to relationships with family, friends, and other loved ones due to use of alcohol or other drugs

The Disease Concept

Addicts continue to seek out and use drugs and alcohol despite negative life consequences. They may wish to stop using and even try to but be unable to do so. The disease concept is rooted in the idea that the addict has an abnormal reaction to a substance to which most people would react differently. For example, a non-alcoholic could have one or two alcoholic beverages and easily stop drinking. An alcoholic, on the other hand, would feel compelled to continue drinking in a way the non-alcoholic could never experience. It is thought that this compulsion is related to abnormalities in the brains of addicts concerning dopamine release and feedback. Thus addicts may use more than one substance or seek out another substance if their drug of choice is not available.

Addiction is an abnormal reaction to what, for others, would be a normal substance (in that it would not set off a compulsion for continuous use despite negative consequences). It is incurable and ultimately fatal. However, as a disease, it is treatable. With the proper treatment and support, thousands of addicts have gone on to live normal and healthy lives in recovery.

The Psychology of Addiction

Addiction may be influenced by the psychological state of the patient. While not necessarily caused by psychological trauma, substance abuse can certainly be a symptom of underlying mental illness; drug use may be the addict's attempt to self-medicate, to escape negative and painful feelings and states of mind beyond his or her control.

Methods of Assessing Addiction

The psychological state of a person can be used as a factor when assessing addiction. By using factors based upon the person's addiction status and their current emotional status in life, the chance of recovery increases. Addiction assessment may include:

- *Patient reports* - Getting reports from the patient on when they are active or non-active in addiction.
- *Using empathy* - This is done when discussing the substance abuse test results with the patient who receives treatment.
- *Biomarkers* - Lab testing is not considered reliable, and should not be used solely to measure a patient's progress. Instead, biomarkers should be used to evaluate the patient's progress.

Purpose of Biomarkers

Biomarkers will allow you to track a patient's recovery process and identify risks of addiction based upon his or her previous psychological patterns and behaviors. Biomarkers can detect occasional or heavy use.

Psychological Elements of Addiction

Understanding the unique psychological aspect of a patient's addiction is important to successful recovery. Without this understanding, recovery is difficult to maintain as the patient's emotions may once again become unmanageable and he or she may once again turn to substance abuse to soothe them. There are three different elements of the psychological aspect of addiction.

- *Sense of powerlessness* - Addiction is often accompanied by feelings of helplessness and powerlessness. The feeling is often experienced after the use of the substance.

- *Sense of hopelessness* – The addict may feel that he or she has no chance of recovery or a better life. Addicts may also feel that their problems are insurmountable.

- *Sense of rage* - People experience rage when they suffer emotional injury; it can fuel substance abuse. The rage may cause the person to show irrational, destructive behavioral patterns. Expression of rage plays a large role in addiction. For some, rage may allow them to take action that will help them. For those who have a substance abuse problem, rage is often turned inwards; instead of redirecting that rage positively towards its cause, they abuse substances to cope.

The Pharmacology of Alcohol and Other Drugs

Each substance has a specific effect on the body and mind. The type, method of administration, and strength of the drug all determine the level of addiction.

Important Pharmacology Terms

- *Drug:* A substance that has a physiological effect on the body when ingested. It may or may not be addictive or produce a state of euphoria.

- *Medicine:* A drug prescribed to a patient to treat a medical condition. It may have a potential for abuse and if so, its use should be monitored.

- *Misuse:* Using a drug in a manner, or for a reason that differs from how it was prescribed. This type of use is unintentional.

- *Abuse:* Using a drug in a manner other than prescribed, with the intention of getting high, such as taking too much.

- *Dependence:* A state that occurs when drug or alcohol abuse has persisted for a prolonged time. The person can become both mentally and physically addicted to the drug.

- *Psychological dependence*: When a person has a strong mental urge to use a drug to experience the effects considered to be pleasant (drug or alcohol used to reach a euphoric state of mind)

- *Physical dependence*: Occurs when a person's body is used to taking the drug, and they start to experience withdrawal symptoms when the drug is no longer present in their system.

- *Cross-dependence*: A person may use another drug form to lessen the withdrawal they are experiencing from their drug of choice.

- *Tolerance:* The body will adjust to a drug over a prolonged time, and the effects will not be the same when taken. Tolerance often leads to taking larger amounts of the substance to try to achieve the same effects.

- *Reverse tolerance*: This can cause a person to become more sensitive to the drug over a period of time, rather than less sensitive. It will cause the substance to have a higher level of impact on the person when taken.

- *Dose:* How much taken at one time or over the course of 24 hours.

- *Half-life*: The amount of time the drug stays present within the body. This level can be affected based upon metabolism and other factors, which differ from the specific half-life of the drug.

- *Lethal dose*: When the dose of a drug taken is too potent and results in death.

- *Therapeutic dose*: The amount of drug needed in order to be effective.

- *Drug interactions*: The way that drugs interact with one another. This includes interactions between street drugs, prescription drugs, and alcohol.

The way the drug is administered can affect its method of action. For example, a drug may be stronger when taken intravenously as opposed to orally. There are different forms of administration for each substance. Abuse of a substance can occur when the method that is traditionally used for the drug is altered. For example, if a drug is transformed into a liquid and injected with a syringe, rather than taken orally as prescribed, it is abused.

Oral Administration

The most common method of drug administration is orally, when the drug comes in pill or capsule form. Some medications that are taken orally have restrictions that make it necessary for the medication to be taken orally. For example, a time-released medication will need to be taken by mouth and cannot be crushed, or the time release action will be disrupted, causing the patient to receive too much medication at once. Other methods of administration are generally used when medication is not available in pill form, when the patient needs a faster-acting medication, or if the patient is unable to swallow the medication properly.

Inhalation

Certain drugs can be taken through inhalation methods, but this is very seldom used as a prescribed form of administration. While the use of marijuana is approved in some states for certain conditions, your patient must provide you with clear documentation of the prescription if this is the case.

Intranasal (Snorting)

Intranasal drug use is also called snorting. This is common among those who abuse oral medications, as this method of administration allows the drug to enter the bloodstream far more quickly than when it is taken orally. While the effects are fast acting, the side-effects can be very dangerous, and in some cases, deadly. Those who use this method of administration can cause severe damage within the sinus cavity; moreover, brain damage can also occur with both short and prolonged usage.

Suppositories

While not all drugs can be taken rectally, certain drugs such as cocaine can be taken through a suppository. The mucus membranes in the rectum area can absorb some drugs quickly. This can be risky because you cannot predict the sensitivity level of the membranes, and the drug can be absorbed much faster, or to a greater extent, than through other forms of administration.

Intravenous (I.V.) Administration

Using a syringe to administer drugs is common among those who use a variety of different substances. With injection, the drugs are supplied directly into the bloodstream, and the effects occur immediately. Some drug users inject the drug in different areas of the body by intramuscular or subcutaneous injection method, as veins and muscles can become damaged with prolonged injections applied to the same areas. These include:

- Intramuscular injections inject the drug right into the muscle.

- Subcutaneous injections inject the drug into the soft tissue under the skin.

When drugs are injected, there are additional risks present. While the risk of overdose is high with this method of administration, the risk of contracting a disease is also increased. This is because if a needle is shared with someone who has a disease, it can be easily spread to the next person. The risk of an infection is also high when using this method, as many drugs require the use of cotton, which can get stuck within the syringe and get under the skin. Infections can also occur due to lack of proper preparation, which creates an unsterile environment.

Eating/Drinking

Administration is also done orally by eating or drinking a substance. Alcohol is most commonly drunk, but certain drugs need to be eaten in order for them to work properly, such as LSD or "magic" mushrooms containing psilocybin.

Toxicology Testing

There are different testing methods that collect information on the type, amount and last use of a drug. There three common toxicology testing methods include urine, blood, and saliva testing. In rare cases, the sweat or the contents of the stomach can be used. However, these are rarely used in toxicology testing involved with addiction.

Urine Testing

A urine sample is collected within a sterilized container, and the container may already have the testing device on it. If the test needs additional screening, it can be sent to a laboratory, which will provide more accurate testing results. This includes the amount of the drug present in the urine and the last time the drug was used. Urine testing must be done within five days of the collected sample, as the drug begins to leave the urine at this time and an accurate test cannot be conducted.

Saliva Testing

A cotton swab is used to take a sample from the mouth. The mucus membranes within the mouth will have traces of the drug, which will then move into the saliva. This testing is done by using the swab on the inside of the cheek, and then enclosing the swab in a sterilized container that will be sent to a lab for testing.

Blood Testing

To perform blood testing, a blood sample is taken from the patient with a syringe. This method of testing is one of the most effective for drugs, as drugs can be detected in the blood much faster than urine and saliva, and they also stay in the blood for longer periods of time. One blood sample is all that is needed, regardless of the amount of drugs being assessed.

Drug testing in any of these forms can be done to check for one specific drug, or to check for up to thirty drugs at one time. The testing method used depends upon the reason or testing. For example, if the test is taken for legal purposes, the examiner will look for a variety of drugs. However, when being used to help with addiction, one specific drug or those in a similar class are the focus.

There are many models of addiction treatment. The perspective of the client and his or her family will often indicate which approach will benefit the addict for the long term. There are numerous types of addictions, from drugs to gambling, from interpersonal relationships to sex. As many different types of addictions exist, there also are many models and theories of addiction. To be successful, the addiction model must blend multidimensional aspects of addiction with various cultural and regional aspects, interpersonal preferences, and family concepts.

Understanding Addiction Models and Theories

To understand models and theories of addiction, the counselor should:

- Have a complete understanding of the models and theories surrounding addiction, and how these affect the patient's addiction and recovery process.

- Develop an understanding of the appropriate models used to treat addiction.

- Master all terms related to theories and concepts involved in addiction.

- Develop an understanding of the proper methods used to evaluate addiction.

- Gain knowledge and understanding of all areas involved within the addiction process, which include the models of psychology, sociology, biology, genetics, and other dispositions.

- Understand the social, economic, and cultural aspects of addiction.

- Evaluate each person's addiction status based upon their social, economic, and cultural stance.

- Understand all of the risk factors involved with addiction.

- Use statistical information gained from research.

Medical Model

The medical model of addiction is well established with most rehabilitation centers. In addition, it is a descriptive model that does not lead to one method of intervention. The outline of this model and the addiction process involves:

- *Genetic predisposition* - The person is genetically predisposed to addiction;

they have one or more family members who are also addicts. This may explain why similar behavior leads to addiction in certain people.

- *Response to addictive chemicals* - The person has a specialized response to substances, which explains why taking a drug is unpleasant or not a compulsion for some people, while it may be one or both or another.

- *Risk factors* - The model takes into account contexts like social environment, preexisting mood disorders, drug availability, and life problems.

- *Practice* – The individual has undergone a trial and error process, experimenting or "learning" how to use the drug and becoming addicted in the process.

- *Change from use to addiction* - This is when behavior changes from occasional use to full-blown addiction, which involves hyposensitation and hedonic dysregulation (the inability to feel good without the drug).

The breadth of the medical model of addiction divides the process of addiction into stages, each of which can be viewed as a target for intervention. This model helps counselors and medical professionals better judge the likelihood and severity of addiction in specific cases; however it does not apply to addictions that do not involve chemical substances.

Cultural Belief Model

The cultural beliefs of a patient must be addressed when providing patient care. Certain behaviors may be attributed to the culture of the patient, and it would be unethical to disrupt any behaviors that are related to culture. Certain expressions can also vary, and all of these different cultural aspects must be considered when first accessing the patient's drug addiction, and then again when creating an effective treatment method for the patient.

Moral Model

Historically, addiction has been seen as a moral failing. Addicts were believed to be morally bereft individuals unable to resist temptation and only treatable spiritually. Today, some in society treat addiction as a character flaw, considering it a moral failing, although this taboo is changing.

The moral model has fallen out of favor because the medical community identifies addiction as a real disease process with a true genetic component. This is a dilemma for many addicts who do not understand this process and feel as if their poor choices are the result of moral failings.

Proponents of the moral model argue that addiction is either caused by a spiritual deficit or is the conscious choice of the addict. Suggested courses of treatment include clerical intervention and moral persuasion or, at the other end of the spectrum, imprisonment and other social consequences of drug use, limiting treatment workers to non-specialists such as clerical workers and law enforcement officials.

Cognitive Model

Unlike biological, social, or emotional addiction models, the cognitive model of addiction focuses on cognition, the mental process that relates to judgment, perception, and reasoning. Here, counselors must find out what core beliefs allow the addict to engage in drug using behavior, both conscious and unconscious. There is no one-size-fits-all approach with this model. The cognitive model of addiction became popular in 2005 and combines addiction treatment with behavioral therapy. This combination attacks false beliefs and teaches the addict skills to deal with stress in a positive manner. Therapies such as cognitive behavioral therapy and dialectical behavioral therapy may be used in conjunction with addiction treatment to help addicts cope with emotions in situations where they would otherwise resort to using.

Bio-Psycho-Social Model

The bio-psycho-social (BPS) model of addiction is an attempt to explain how addiction starts, continues, and persists. This model helps counselors establish a treatment program. The biological factors of the BPS model involve genetics and chemical changes that occur from drug use, and are viewed as the primary cause for the addiction. The BPS model expands to include emotional (psychological) and social aspects of addiction. This model involves family matters, poverty, crime, opportunity, mental disorders, and the influence of friends. Critics of this model feel that it is too broad and does not really give a target to treat and attack. Practical addiction treatment tends to blend the BPS model with the medical model. Along with medications, treatment is often more successful.

Temperance Model

Often confused with the moral approach, the temperance model actually focuses on the drug or substance itself rather than the addict. The temperance model developed during the prohibition movement in the United States during the nineteenth century; it condemns the addictive substance and its potential to harm people and social institutions rather than the addict him- or herself.

Psychological or Characterological Model

According to this model, addiction is caused by a psychological abnormality exhibited by addicts: the "addictive personality." Addictive personalities are characterized by self-centeredness, low self-esteem, impulsiveness, low tolerance for stress, tendencies toward manipulation, and a desire for power or control. Treatment under this model includes psychotherapy and social support. Treatment specialists like social workers and psychotherapists help addicts develop self-esteem and impulse control, learn how to set appropriate boundaries, and learn or improve interpersonal skills.

Social Education Model

According to the social education model, addiction is a learned behavior. This integrative approach is based on principles of classical and operant conditioning, and it views addiction as the result of social influence or of the addict imitating behavior and then ongoing cognitive processes. Proponents of the social education model believe that it identifies precursors to addiction—learned behaviors—and then ongoing reinforcement of it through operant conditioning.

This model cites poor socialization, poor modeling and limited coping mechanisms and skills or lack of them altogether as the causes of addiction. Treatment includes training in impulse control and other social skills, cognitive exercises and reconditioning, appropriate and realistic goal setting, and appropriate behavioral modeling overseen by cognitive and behavioral counselors. Peer groups are often utilized in the social education model.

Biological Model

The biological model of addiction is based upon genetic factors that influence addiction. Genetics, biochemistry, and metabolism all play a role in biological addiction factors. Similar to the reaction that some people have to certain foods, some people may be unable to tolerate alcohol, even when consumed in small amounts. Their bodies will act adversely to the substance, and behavioral issues will occur. Women tend to have a lower tolerance to alcohol then men. When addiction occurs based on genetic factors, signs of addiction often show before the substance is used. Signs are seen at a young age, which include violent behaviors, impulsive behaviors, and deficient social skills. The enzyme MYOB may be lower in the brain of those who are susceptible to alcohol abuse due to their genetic disposition.

Genetics Theory

Genetics, or addictive inheritance theory, identifies the genetic factors of addiction separately from environmental factors. While there are many environmental components of addiction, studies have shown that the children of alcoholic parents later adopted into non-alcoholic families have a greater risk of alcoholism than the general population. Furthermore, certain populations are at a higher risk for addictive inheritance. Due to a genetic predisposition to a deficiency in acetaldehyde production—the enzyme that degrades alcohol—they are hypersensitive to its effects. Finally, sons are more likely than daughters to inherit alcoholism.

Exposure Theory

Exposure theory assumes that addiction will eventually occur after the regular use of a substance. Due to drug use, the body undergoes metabolic changes; in order to avoid withdrawal, the body therefore demands higher and more frequent amounts of a drug. According to this theory, the drug is mimicking the body's natural painkillers, endorphins, and thus reducing the body's ability to produce endorphins naturally, causing chemical dependency and ultimately, addiction.

Conditioning Theory

According to conditioning theory, addiction is reinforced by drug use itself. Given the rewarding effect of the drug, the substance itself controls the user's behavior; the user becomes conditioned to use the substance—becomes addicted to it—due to its rewarding effect.

Adaption Theory

According to adaption theory, environmental, social, and psychological factors influence addiction and contribute to its potential, such as beliefs about the drug itself, subjective emotional experiences, and other internal and external dynamics. Adaptation theorists have investigated the psychodynamics of drug reliance; they also believe that some causes of addiction are problems in childhood, low self-esteem, and other psychological problems.

Addiction treatment and recovery tackles two groups: those who experience addiction alone, those who suffer from both addiction and mental health disorders.

Mental Health Concept

Approaching a patient's mental health is part of an addiction treatment program. Research has shown that proper treatment for patients at mental health facilities frequently must include addiction recovery methods. Furthermore, people with severe mental illnesses only experience success in addiction recovery one-half of the time.

Concept of Recovery in Addiction

Recovery from addiction is the ongoing process of transformational change allowing the addict to stop using and develop new skills to maintain a manageable life. Recovery is generally supported by a planned treatment program. With ongoing research, methods of addiction treatment have grown and diversified; applying diverse treatment techniques in an integrated, interdisciplinary fashion supports the recovery of patients in treatment. Using a variety of methods, counselors can tailor treatment plans to meet the needs of their patients and provide long-term positive effects. Counselors review the patient's current recovery process in the framework of the recovery concept, developing new patient recovery plans when appropriate. Furthermore, the recovery process must be adjusted whenever it becomes ineffective for the patient.

The addiction advocacy movement developed in order to provide recovery to patients by involving their families. Connecting with families as part of a treatment program helps patients achieve long-term recovery; patients receive support from their family members while undergoing the treatment process.

Recovering from addiction requires taking a patient's mental health into consideration, whether mental health problems present due to drug abuse or for other reasons. The mental health status of the patient is evaluated prior to starting the recovery process. By treating the patient's mental health, the chance of a successful recovery increases. Therapy helps the patient gain the skills needed for long-term recovery.

Recovery is a personalized process. As it progresses, patients become more aware of what they must do to keep their recovery on track. Each person undergoing the recovery process is responsible for his or her own recovery; patients should use the tools provided by the counselor or group their own time while going through the recovery process.

The concept of recovery had first only taken into account the aspects involved in complete recovery. However, knowledge based upon partial recovery, and the concepts involved in this process have grown. Full recovery and partial recovery treatment options are now used in conjunction for those in recovery, and this combination of the two concepts has increased the promise of higher success rates.

Prevention

Prevention groups are a groups of individuals who work together in order to educate a target group about drug use. The groups included in the process of intervention include the general population, at-risk individuals, and high-risk individuals. The main goal is to prevent drug use entirely; however prevention groups also to address abuse if it should occur by catching it while in the early stages. In communities with widespread drug use, preventative measures should be taken in order to avert further progression. Groups can also take action to restore the health of drug users, including by providing education on drug resistance, decision making skills, and conflict resolution.

Preventive Methods

- Reducing the available supply of drugs and alcohol through appropriate measures, including legal assistance.

- Reducing the amount of demand present for drugs and alcohol by providing those in the community with appropriate treatment methods.

- Continuing development of treatment centers to improve level of care.

Primary Prevention

Primary prevention is used for young people or those with little to no history of drug/alcohol abuse. It is applied by:

- Promoting abstinence from drugs and alcohol.

- Teaching refusal skills to those who haven't used.

- Increasing "usage" policies, such as age limit to buy alcohol.

- Providing education on the dangers associated with drug and alcohol use.

- Promoting safe alternatives by offering community activities to the younger generation.

Secondary Prevention

Secondary prevention is used to help addicts once early usage is detected by way of the HALT Theory. This includes:

- Using intervention methods to stop drug/substance use and abuse.

- Providing education on the risks, dangers, and other negative factors associated with drug abuse.

- Providing skill-building techniques to help clients refrain from further use.

Tertiary Prevention

Tertiary prevention is used when drug or alcohol use and abuse has become progressive and promotes healing of the mind and body. It includes:

- Applying intervention processes to stop drug use and encourage recovery.

- Sending the patient to an appropriate detox facility to stop use safely.

- Using treatment center after detox to help ensure proper recovery process.

- Using a specialized approach to treatment that includes desensitizing users to triggers, such as people, places, things, and actions.

- Using pharmaceutical approaches to help recovery success.

- Creating a solid aftercare program for treatment after the initial program is complete.

- Teaching the Twelve-Step principles to the patient in order to prepare him or her for aftercare.

Intervention

Intervention is a process in which a group of people work together in order to interrupt addiction. This offers recovering addicts several options that can be used to stop the process of addiction. Also, intervention can prevent the individual from hitting rock bottom, and it works to reorient those who have lost touch with reality during the addiction process. The intervention process involves meeting with the family and significant others of the addict, whom a counselor will assisted through the process. The process is successful when applied using detached caring.

Steps of Intervention

Several steps are involved in the process of intervention. These include:

- Gathering the intervention team together.

- Making lists of incidents and occurrences that are of concern regarding the addiction.

- Designating one individual to be the chairperson for the group, who is often the person closest to the addict or the counselor.

- Determining the reading order process that will be used during the intervention.

- Developing a list of firm, realistic steps that will be used by each team member during the intervention.

- Gathering information on available treatment options to present to the addict during the intervention process. The list must be created taking different factors into consideration, such as affordable treatment options and locations of open treatment centers.

- Deciding upon the date and time that the intervention will take place.

Benefits of Intervention

While an intervention is not always successful for the addict, the process can still be successful for those involved. This is because it offers different benefits which include:

- Coming together for the first time as a family since the addiction started.

- Learning techniques that family members can use for self-help.

- Stopping denial of the addiction in both family members and the addict.

- Learning as a group how to stop enabling addiction.

Treatment

The treatment process must be viewed as continuous. The treatment used for recovery is determined based upon certain criteria that the patient meets. To determine the level of addiction present and place the addict into the appropriate category, the counselor must decide which category applies. These include:

- *Non-user* - This person does not or has not used substances.

- *Moderate and non-problematic user* - This person uses some substances occasionally, but the use has not had a negative effect on the patient's life so far.

- *Heavy and non-problematic user* - This person uses substances heavily, but hasn't had negative effects occur with health or life.

- *Heavy with moderate problems* - This person uses often and has had a few problems occur as a result of the use.

- *Heavy with serious problems* - This person uses substances very often, and has had many negative events occur due to use.

- *Dependent and addicted with life and health problems* - This person is unable to stop drugs due to physical and mental addiction, and the use and abuse of substances has caused issues in the patient's personal life, as well as had a negative effect on his or her health.

Steps for Treatment

Providing treatment for addiction requires the following steps in order for it to be effective:

1. *Identify:* Screen the areas of the patient's life affected by the addiction and identify the level of addiction present in the patient.

2. *Assessment:* Collect information from the patient, and those involved in the patient's treatment plan, to identify the patient's strengths, weaknesses, and treatment goals. Use the information gained during the assessment to create a long-term treatment plan for the patient.

3. *Stabilize:* Stop addiction to the substance(s) using appropriate methods. Some methods include; detox and use of pharmaceutical alternatives in order to help stop addiction and create a secure recovery foundation.

4. *Rehabilitate:* Determine the proper long-term treatment program for the patient based upon the issues detected during the assessment and development of the overall treatment plan.

Types of Rehab Programs

Rehabilitation (rehab) programs are all designed to help the addict stop the process of addiction, but there are different forms of programs available. These include:

- *Co-occurring treatment centers:* These facilities offer treatment to patients who have mental health and substance abuse issues.

- *Inpatient facilities:* These units are designed to treat patients who stay at the facility over the entire course of treatment. Treatment generally lasts from one to six months.

- *Outpatient facilities:* These centers offer the same type of care as inpatient rehabilitation facilities, except the patient leaves the facility and goes home after the treatment is completed each day.

- *Aftercare program:* Typically used for patients that have successfully completed an inpatient or outpatient rehab program. These programs may be used for patients who experience addiction without life issues, and when it is determined that addiction may be stopped with a less aggressive treatment program.

Each of these programs work to initiate the initial recovery process. The initial process is vital, but there must also be further preventative measures used to stop relapse from occurring once the treatment program is complete. These preventative measures are offered to the patient during the time of treatment. They include:

- Identifying triggers that could lead to substance abuse again.

- Determining which coping methods can be used in order to stop a relapse when a trigger occurs.

- Addressing any personal problems related to the addiction in the patient.

- Helping the patient work through problems to help with recovery.

Goal Setting

An important part of any treatment program is to set goals with the patient. Goals are based upon the patient's desires, and are created using realistic measures. Goal setting offers several benefits which include:

- Makes the recovery more obtainable by creating steps to reach the goal.

- Reviews goals frequently in order to maintain recovery and stay on track.

- Shares success stories when goals are reached to maintain progress.

Drug Substitution with Alternative Pharmaceuticals

Some patients may benefit from replacement pharmaceuticals, which are designed to assist the patient in the early stages of recovery. When using a substitute drug, review the pharmaceutical used and be sure that the patient is using it properly. This will increase the chances of success at the treatment center and afterwards.

Addiction Therapy

Addiction therapy is offered during treatment in three different forms.

1. *Individual therapy:* Provided to the patient on a one-on-one basis. This offers patients the ability to speak about personal issues and learn coping techniques to help them work through barriers to a successful recovery.

2. *Group therapy:* Offers the patient the ability to participate in a group setting with peers who also face addiction. This gives the patient the opportunity to relate to others with similar issues, as well as to develop a support team.

3. *Family therapy:* Used to help the addict and family members work through issues that may have occurred during active use. This type of therapy also helps members of the family to understand the addiction process, as well as to obtain skills to assist the patient through the recovery by using supportive techniques and eliminating denial.

Self-Help Approaches

A successful recovery is based upon the addict taking control of the recovery process and making it a personal goal. There are several programs used to help the patient develop self-help techniques, which increase the chances of a successful recovery. The main area of focus used within the various self-help groups is the Twelve Steps, which were created as the original principles for Alcoholics Anonymous. These steps are also used for other groups as a self-help recovery tool.

Common Twelve Step Rehabilitation Programs

Various rehabilitation programs use these principles, but the steps have changed to fit the needs of the different programs. The Twelve Steps are used for both addicts and family members of addicts who are working as part of the recovery treatment process. Twelve Step fellowships are independent from treatment centers, although they may organize visits to hold meetings and introduce patients to Twelve Step programs. Some centers encourage patients to organize their own Twelve Step meetings and study relevant literature; it can also be helpful for patients at inpatient rehabilitation centers to be taken to meetings outside the facilities. Some common Twelve Step programs include:

- *Alcoholics Anonymous (AA):* A fellowship of men and women who come together for support in recovery. The only requirement to join is the desire to stop drinking. AA originally focused on alcohol abuse, but many members also struggle with drug abuse and discuss it as part of their sobriety.

- *Narcotics Anonymous (NA):* A fellowship of men and women who come together for support in recovery. The only requirement to join is the desire to stop using. NA focuses on addiction itself rather than any specific drug; it also specifies that alcohol is a drug.

- *Al-Anon:* A fellowship for family members and friends of addicts who are trying to understand how they can manage their own lives while suffering from the consequences of the addiction of their loved one.

- *Ala-Teen:* A fellowship for younger family members of addicts that is based on the same principles as Al-Anon.

Additional Self-Help Groups

- *Rational Recovery:* This group of addicts supports each other through the use of rational recreation therapy. The therapy is based upon the use of rational thinking as the way to recovery.

- *Moderate Management:* This group is not for addictive drinkers. Rather, it is for non-addictive drinkers who face life issues as a result of their drinking patterns.

- *The Secular Organization of Sobriety:* This group uses the one-day-at-a-time method of thinking. Members of the group face addiction to both drugs and alcohol.

- *Women for Sobriety:* This is a spiritual-based group that uses the Twelve Steps, along with some AA principles. The main focus is to use positive emotion as the way to stay sober.

Knowledge of Addiction

The experiential practicum in knowledge of addiction requires that the counselor gain proper knowledge. In order to provide the patient with the right care, several areas must be examined during the initial intervention, treatment, and preventative processes used for the patient. The areas of addiction that must be addressed include:

- Identify the type of addiction that is present.

- Determine the level of readiness to change that the patient displays.

- Identify any problems and beliefs related to the addiction.

- Provide several levels of patient care to the patient, and individual, group, and family therapy should be used in conjunction when appropriate.

- Advocate for patient care.

- Take active participation in patient's treatment plan.

- Make referrals to appropriate professionals when needed for additional treatment.

- Keep an accurate record of patient care.

- Work as a team with others involved within the patient's treatment plan.

- Act as a positive role model for those receiving the care.

- Provide the patient and public with information on preventative measures that can be taken in order to help prevent addiction.

- Continue education process by keeping up with the most recent information provided regarding addiction, effective treatment, and other areas involving treating patients with addiction problems.

The skills acquired while working towards a degree must be applied to each case during the initial phases of treatment, as well as while going through the treatment process. Any changes made to the processes should be evaluated and then applied to the patient's care program.

Alcoholism and Substance Abuse Counseling
(150 Hours)

Health Issues

HIV/AIDS

HIV (Human Immunodeficiency Virus) is a contagious virus that attacks the body's immune system. It is spread via blood and other bodily fluids. It lives within the cells of the body and dies once it is exposed to oxygen. Anyone can get HIV, whether or not they are an addict and regardless of their sexual orientation, gender, race, ethnicity, job, or income level. Intravenous (IV) or injecting drug users are at a high risk of contracting HIV if they share needles. HIV is also sexually transmitted; individuals who engage in unprotected sex are at high risk.

Transmission occurs through:

- *Sexual activity* – During sexual intercourse, HIV may be transmitted through semen, vaginal fluids, and blood. Tearing in the anus, rectum, or vagina due to anal or vaginal intercourse can heighten the risk of transmission. HIV can also be transmitted during oral intercourse.

- *Sharing needles* – HIV can be transmitted between intravenous drug users who share "works," including needles, cotton, water, and "cookers" (bottle caps, spoons, and other containers to dissolve drugs).

- *Mother to child transmission* – mothers can transmit HIV to their children during pregnancy, childbirth, and breastfeeding, although the risks of this are greatly lowered with treatment.

Those with STDs in the form of lesions, cuts, and open sores also have a higher risk of contracting HIV, as these wounds can facilitate the transmission of the disease from contact with the bodily fluids identified above.

The HIV virus is most easily transmitted when a person is first infected. Once the HIV virus is passed to another individual, it spreads rapidly throughout the immune system. A newly infected person may experience flu-like symptoms during this period of acute infection, which lasts from two to four weeks. This period is followed by a term of clinical latency or chronic HIV infection, where the person may experience no symptoms for a period of several years, but is still able to transmit the virus.

HIV is not curable, but it is treatable. Antiretroviral therapy (ART) can help persons with HIV live for many decades in clinical latency. A person living with HIV is considered to have progressed to AIDS (Acquired Immunodeficiency Syndrome) once suppression of the immune system occurs or once he or she develops an opportunistic illness (an illness that takes advantage of the weakened immune system). Without treatment, a patient's life expectancy with AIDS is about three years; if he or she has an opportunistic illness, it is about one year.[1]

Risky Sexual Behavior and STDs

Risky sexual behavior can increase the chances of contacting a sexually transmitted disease (STD). Drug addicts may have engaged in risky behavior throughout their addiction such as offering sex in exchange for drugs.

Prevention of STD Transmission

Stopping drug use with treatment lowers the risk of transmitting various STDs. This is done by reducing the amount of risky behavior in the patient. In order to reduce the risk, the patient must be provided with a treatment plan that focuses on treating drug addiction rather than preventing STD transmission. While stopping both behaviors is important, without an active addiction, the probability of contracting an STD is greatly reduced. The patient should also be educated on the exact way in which HIV transition occurs, as well as other STDs. Drug use, active substance abuse, STDs, and mental health are intertwined. Often, if each factor is not addressed during the treatment process, it will cause another factor to react, and the process will start over again.

Risk Reduction Counseling

Risk reduction counseling uses substance-abuse prevention to stop the spreading of HIV/AIDS and STDs. Counselors educate patients about the transmission of HIV/AIDS and STDs during risky behaviors like IV drug use and unsafe sexual activity. During this time, any questions that the patient may have will be answered. The patient should also be offered factual information regarding the transmission of HIV/AIDS and STDs during the counseling session.

HIV/AIDS education helps the patient understand the importance of change to prevent contracting this serious disease or, if the patient is already living with HIV, to begin proper treatment for it. During this counseling session, the risk reduction counselor offers information on developing skills for change. For example, many

---

[1] HIV/AIDS, "About HIV/AIDS," Centers for Disease Control and Prevention, http://www.cdc.gov/hiv/basics/whatishiv.html (last updated January 16, 2015).

patients lack a proper support group, which can result in use of drugs. If their peers use syringes during the process of using drugs, they will be more likely to use syringes, too. Patients need to learn coping skills to avoid their old environments; otherwise, relapse, more advanced use, and the likelihood of contracting and/or transmitting HIV/AIDS and/or another STD increase.

Education

To educate the recovering addict, the counselor should provide information on the risks associated with injection. This education will not only be provided to people who are in the early stages of recovery, but it should also be provided to those are actively using. This process is done by encouraging cessation of substance use and the use of clean syringes. While it is not always possible for the addict to stop substance use completely, by providing the patient with the proper education, he or she could reduce the risk of contracting HIV or another STD.

- *When the Addict is Actively Using:*
  - Provide proper coping skills.
  - Give information on ways to build the immune system.
  - Discuss the benefits of exercise.
  - Teach self-exams to detect issues regarding patient's health.
- *Offer External Resources to Patient*
  - Housesitting
  - Residential program
  - Home healthcare
  - Support groups
  - Info and treatment options that are available

The Counselor's Role

- Always treat patients with STDs, especially HIV or AIDS, with the same care and respect as those who do not have an infectious disease.
- Provide support to the patient in order to help them cope with their disease. This is especially important for those just learning that they have the virus. Offer the patient educational information, such as pamphlets and brochures.

- Discuss different treatment options available for the patient regarding the disease. Treatment must be focused upon recovery, but can be used to discuss diseases. This is done in a way that will help the patient to feel hope for the future. When a patient feels hopeless, it can lead to relapse.

- Offer the patient the steps needed for behavioral changes. While the HIV virus cannot be eliminated, providing a patient with useful information needed for behavioral change will help prevent relapse. Additionally, this will reduce the likelihood of actively using again and the possibility of spreading the virus to other people who have drug addiction problems.

- Someone who has an incurable STD may be less likely to take behavioral change seriously, so provide the patient with information on the serious nature of the disease in order to offset the possibility that they may contact a worse condition in the future. Remind them that while the disease may be incurable, it can be treated.

Preventing STD Infection

Case workers and alcoholism and substance abuse counselors must provide the patient with tentative methods of avoiding STD infection. These include:

- Proper education on different types of STDs and how they affect a person's life, well-being, health and future.

- Instruction on the use of standard precautions as a part of everyday life. The patient may not be aware of which precautions they should take in order to reduce the risk of transmission. Precautions make the patient less likely to encounter a STD and able to better protect themselves.

- Ensure that the treatment used is one that is aimed towards both recovery from drugs and alcohol and prevention of STDs.

- Take the steps needed to identify relapse and put a stop to it. By working with the patient, you will be able to identify different trigger cues or behaviors that indicate when a relapse is going to occur.

Helping Patients Stay in Recovery

The therapeutic techniques the counselor offers to patients must help them stay in recovery. Initially, the counselor must offer the patient encouragement, or the hope that his or her life will improve with recovery. Furthermore, the counselor should bond with the patient, confirming to the patient that he or she has support in the recovery process.

The counselor helps set goals for therapy both at a personal and group level. Individual goals should be based upon the patient's wishes for her or his recovery; the group should have one common goal.

A group therapy session focuses on discussing events and feelings, helping patients get accustomed to emotional expression. The counselor should be prepared to assist patients in addressing unexpected, subconscious feelings and fears that can arise, particularly following a period of heavy use that has masked emotions. Ultimately, patients will be better able to recognize their emotions and trust their feelings.

In facilitating the group, counselors help patients develop social skills within the context of group activities (like role play). Group activities also help patients learn about their own behavior; by witnessing the behavior of other group members, patients become better able to recognize it in themselves, mimicking positive behavior and developing plans to change negative behavior. The counselor assists in facilitating this personal development and developing behavior plan changes.

Any group will face the challenge of conflict. Counselors can help patients develop appropriate conflict resolution skills by acting as mentors and creating an environment where patients learn to express their feelings in a positive way, leading to resolution of the conflict. Furthermore, this kind of positive environment will help create an atmosphere of trust, enabling addicts to develop trust for others as they feel empowered to discuss their emotions in a secure group.

Trust in others is necessary for developing a support group of understanding peers, an essential tool of recovery. The group and counselor are an integral part of this support group. The counselor may also encourage patients to reach out to loved ones they may have lost contact with due to addiction, in order to begin repairing those relationships. Other forms of outreach include helping others; not only is this part of the principles of the Twelve Steps, but it will also help boost patients' self-esteem. A person in recovery has much to offer a struggling addict.

Finally, the group context gives patients an opportunity for education about addiction, both through the experiences of other members and more formally, through presentations from outside experts.

Group Skills Exhibited by Counselors

In general, counselors provide positive support to group members, ongoing education about recovery and tools for staying clean, and work to create group cohesion, including through conflict resolution, preventing the formation of small groups (or cliques) within the larger one, and dealing with difficult group members appropriately.

Should a group member relapse, the counselor must address the situation. If appropriate, the group should address it together.

Crisis Intervention and Resolution

In case of a crisis, the counselor must secure a safe environment for the patient and other group members, depending on the severity and nature of the crisis. Determine the cause of the crisis, such as conflict or loss of family member; then offer support to the patient and attempt to help find a resolution. In the longer term, help the patient to create a plan for action during the time of distress. Counselors should also offer the patient additional resources to cope with cause of crisis.

Immediate Crisis Intervention Steps

1. Initiate the intervention.

2. Offer hope to the patient with positive statements.

3. Provide support to the recovering addict.

4. Provide a solution to problem immediately.

5. Give feedback to the patient in a positive manner.

Individual counseling offers patients the ability to work on a one-on-one basis with a counselor. This form of treatment can offer the recovering addict the ability to express deep issues and concerns that he or she may not feel comfortable expressing in a group setting. The counselor can also provide the patient with a sense of security during individual counseling, which will help patients acknowledge and address issues they may be afraid to confront. Individual counseling allows behaviors and traits displayed by the member during the group session to be specifically addressed.

Counselor Services

As active listeners, counselors provide the patient with feedback, ask questions, develop goals with the patient, and reflect on the patient's thoughts and emotions. Part of active listening is offering empathy. Counselors should attempt to identify with clients, or "put themselves in their shoes," in order to develop a true understanding of their addiction and related problems.

Some key actions demonstrate active listening to the client. Using verbal and physical cues (in the form of body language) shows a patient that you are actively listening to what he or she is telling you. Paraphrasing the client's words, or repeating important information he or she provides, enables the client to better reflect on his or her thoughts. Encouraging frequent reflection on thoughts, feelings, and what has been learned through counseling allows the patient to develop his or her own emotional connection with the counselor. Offering simple solutions to complex conflicts the patient presents can help resolve those conflicts; furthermore, counselors can teach coping skills so that clients can deal with complex situations or challenges in a more positive manner. At the same time, however, counselors should avoid interpretation. Allow the patient to have freedom of expression; do not assume that you understand the client's experience.

Finally, ask questions, and leave questions open-ended in order to encourage the patient to explain things in further detail; this allows you both to develop a deeper understanding of the issues at hand. At the end of the session, summarize what was discussed, what was learned, and how to expand on these topics during the next session.

Goal of Individual Counseling

The overall goal of individual counseling is to address the issues contributing to addiction and then to slowly work through each with an overall goal in mind of creating lasting change. The steps used in process of change will allow the counselor to work with the patient to help him or her recognize the need for change in certain areas of life, start the process of creating a plan for change, implement the change, and then, through recovery from abuse and underlying issues, allow for lasting change.

Certain issues need to be addressed when working with patients during individual counseling. Some recovering addicts have certain cultural beliefs, outlooks on addiction, and personal beliefs that can affect the treatment plan. Taking each difference into consideration and monitoring the effectiveness of the overall treatment plan throughout the process will allow changes to be made when necessary to make the plan effective.

Methods of Individual Therapy

There are a few different methods used in individual therapy. The method used is based upon the patient's unique needs.

1. *Talk therapy:* This form of treatment creates a secure environment where the patient can discuss his or her issues in confidence, and the therapist can offer encouragement, support, and positive coping techniques.

2. *Cognitive therapy*: This type of therapy uses different methods to encourage the patient to take part in activities designed to change overall thinking, behavior, and ways of handling issues throughout the recovery process.

3. *Hypnosis/EMDR (Eye Movement Desensitization and Reprocessing):* While less commonly used, these approaches are designed to change the patient's subconscious mind though special techniques. Some professionals feel these two methods can offer lasting change, because they can help the patient deal with issues they were not aware existed.

Initial Assessment

During the initial assessment, the drug and alcohol counselor will consider different factors in order to determine the patient's best interest. Certain special-needs patients, such as those with mental health issues, may need to be assessed more thoroughly because of certain issues with truth regarding recovery, and the risk of relapse due to the patient stopping his or her medication. With the use of the assessment, the counselor can examine the patient's current and prior history of use, methods for recovery, and what techniques the patient responded to in the past.

Individual counseling may be short- or long-term, based upon the patient's particular case. Generally, the use of drug and alcohol counseling will be provided to the patient until he or she has made substantial progress in the recovery. After this, regular maintenance therapy may be used in order to help the patient to cope with life troubles, as well as to re-examine recovery.

The Attributes of an Individual Counselor

Knowledge

Counselors help clients determine treatment goals through the process of counseling. Essential to the collaborative process of counseling is sensitivity to the individual circumstances of a client, including personality, family and loved ones, and social and cultural context. Skilled counselors integrate various addiction counseling models as applicable and appropriate in care for individuals, couples, families, groups, and significant others. In successful individual counseling, the counselor establishes a supportive, authentic, empathetic, and respectful relationship with the client.

A counselor must demonstrate specific competencies. These include knowledge of the counselor's role and counseling actions and strategies. Counselors also must be knowledgeable about specific tactics in working directly with clients. Finally, counselors should have a strong background in applicable recovery-related theory, literature, and research.

Understanding the role of the counselor means understanding definitions of warmth, respect, genuineness, concreteness, and empathy. A good counselor is aware of the therapeutic uses of power and authority. He or she can identify typical reactions and differentiate them from a serious crisis; likewise, counselors understand the differences between crisis intervention and other kinds of therapeutic intervention.

More practically, addiction counselors have a strong knowledge of addiction counseling approaches and strategies, including assessment and treatment planning; how to apply appropriate strategies based on the client's treatment plan; and how to determine basic life skills and develop them in a patient. It is essential for counselors to develop strategies to prevent relapse with their clients; understanding appropriate behavioral, cognitive, and even pharmacological interventions to prevent relapse is imperative.

Counselors should be aware of and adhere to confidentiality laws, rules, and regulations.

In working with clients, counselors provide the individualized attention to understand a client's history, goals, and motivational level; this understanding is the first step in determining a client's prognosis and developing a treatment plan.

Counselors must recognize the behaviors and cognition consistent with the development, maintenance, and attainment of treatment goals; understand the assessment methods to measure progress toward positive change; and be aware of those client behaviors counterproductive to the recovery process. Essential to these three factors is a strong understanding of the client's traditional coping strategies: without understanding the failed tactics the client has traditionally taken, it is impossible to help him or her develop new strategies and instill necessary behavioral change.

Teaching recovery-related skills and perspectives is part of the counselor's job, as is supporting positive behavior. Framing the relationship with the client in the broader context of treatment and engagement stages-of-change models organizes the scope of the treatment process.

As a client undergoes change throughout the recovery process, crisis is a possibility. The counselor assists clients in resolving crises. Counselors are positioned to distinguish between what clients are able to accomplish on their own in order to resolve crises versus what requires intervention by counselor, family, or significant others the client's support system. Keep in mind that while there are roles for the client's support system in resolving crises, those crises may in fact have been triggered by family or other major figures in the client's life.

Understanding a client's broader, culture-specific social context, helps the counselor further individualize recovery strategy. For the above strategies to be of any worth counselors must take the client's specific life circumstances, including cultural influences, into account in order to assess his or her responsiveness: not every client will respond to every strategy, nor is every life skill appropriate in every cultural context.

Furthermore, the impact of culture on substance use is important. For example, some cultures may use alcohol as part of cultural or religious ceremonies; it is important to develop specific coping strategies for these specific situations. Likewise, other cultures may strongly object to the disease model; the counselor may face particular challenges in working with these clients and/or their families. Hence an awareness of cultural perspectives not only on addiction but on health in general is important in addiction counseling; researching and understanding alternative, culturally-sensitive methodologies for encouraging clients in recovery is the responsibility of the counselor. Thus, counselors should have some knowledge of family and social systems theory (the relationships between social and family systems of the client), among other social theories.

In addition to social theory, counselors should be aware of current counseling theory, treatment and practice literature related to substance use and recovery; current research on client-specific differences in addiction patterns; relapse prevention theory and practice; and addiction-related cognitive and behavioral therapy (including dialectical behavioral therapy) literature. A knowledge of the literature studying the relationship between addiction and spirituality is useful. Theory and literature examining how both family support and positive, recovery-related life skills affect treatment should also be included here.

Addiction counselors should also have a general knowledge of basic psychological theory such as post-traumatic stress and other relevant psychiatric disorders. Those applicable to counseling may include transference, counter-transference, and projective identification, and literature related to client motivation.

Finally, given the impact of substance abuse on the lives of many addicts, counselors must understand how infectious diseases are transmitted and prevented and the relationship between lifestyles and infectious diseases. Counselors should have a current knowledge of harm reduction concepts, research, and methods as they relate to addiction and substance abuse.

Skills

Counselors must be able to judge client readiness for change. They must be able to assess client behaviors (and re-assess them to check for progress), including using assessment tools to determine client's initial level of life skills. Assessments also include a client's support system and his or her immediate safety and potential for harm to self or others. Counselors must check for issues of confidentiality that may be part of crisis response. Overall, counselors must judge and assess client response to therapeutic intervention and client progress in treatment, providing feedback.

At the start of treatment, counselors must focus on individualizing treatment plans by using intervention strategies appropriately; recognizing a client's specific strengths; addressing issues that could affect a client's progress in treatment, including reticence, ambivalence, and resistance; and reinforcing positive client behaviors with behavior and cognitive methods. Counselors must identify and document positive change in the client throughout the course of treatment.

Essential to successful treatment is formulating and documenting concise, descriptive, and measurable treatment outcome goals. Counselors should be able to observe and document client progress in an objective manner and carry out ongoing monitoring of the client's behavior and progress to assess consistency with the desired treatment outcomes.

Part of treatment is teaching the client to identify goals and formulate action plans; teaching appropriate life skills and why they affect treatment outcomes; showing how negative behaviors impede treatment progress; teaching conflict resolution, decision-making, and problem-solving skills; and promoting the maintenance of health through activities framed in a client's social and cultural experience. Counselors should also teach clients how to understand and express feelings.

Taking that specific experience into account extends into developing client-specific strategies taking into account a client's own psycho-social factors. Here, the counselor must understand how the client's family and social circumstances affect the treatment process, and he or she must engage the client's family and/or loved ones in the treatment process when possible. Furthermore, counselors should be sensitive to using culturally appropriate counseling strategies and practicing culturally sensitive communication, including regarding sexuality.

Important **communication** skills include practicing active listening (see above), particularly empathy; authentically conveying warmth and respect; and motivating and encouraging clients, or appropriately using authority in pursuit of treatment goals. Finally, counselors must use the appropriate techniques in interviewing and engaging with clients (and their families). Counselors must also take steps to assist in crisis resolution. Counselors should make any referrals as necessary and clearly explain to the client or family why a referral is preferable.

Attitudes

Counselors must demonstrate respect for the client and his or her experience, while maintaining therapeutic optimism, patience, and perseverance. Counselors work with clients to establish realistic recovery goals; as such, counselors should appreciate the contribution clients make in this collaborative process. While an addiction counselor plays a major role in an addict's treatment process, however, clients must ultimately assume responsibility for their own recovery.

Recovery is more than just eliminating the symptoms of active addiction, such as substance abuse; counselors should recognize the benefits of a life in recovery and be able to communicate those benefits to the client, in the context of their constructive helping relationship. Recovery is a gradual process, so counselors should appreciate that progress in recovery comes in incremental changes and communicate that attitude to the client.

To help the client progress in the recovery process, counselors should remain flexible and be willing to adapt treatment strategies in keeping with the client's specific circumstances and individual needs. This includes remaining accepting and non-judgmental regarding differences in values and culture. Counselors should remain open to discussions about health and sexuality while demonstrating sensitivity and compassion.

Counselors should remain respectful of the contribution of a client's family and significant others to the recovery process; at the same time, counselors should recognize the limitations of confidentiality on the need for those significant figures to be involved in recovery.

Counselors should stay calm and confident during crises—such as a relapse—and recognize these situations as opportunities for growth.

Counselors should retain professional objectivity at all times and be aware and accepting of their own limitations, both professional and personal. At the same time, the counselor, as a leading figure in the client's treatment process, has the opportunity to demonstrate a healthy lifestyle.

Vocational Rehabilitation

Vocational rehabilitation allows the recovering addict to overcome barriers to accessing and maintaining employment or a useful occupation. This may require several mental health professionals like disability advisers and career counselors.

Techniques used For Vocational Rehabilitation

- Goal setting
- Intervention planning
- Providing of health advice and promotion

- Support for self-management of recovery

- Psychosocial interventions

- Career counseling, job analysis, and placement services

- Functional capacity evaluations

Determining Rehabilitation Readiness

A recovering addict will show readiness for vocational rehabilitation when he or she:
- Recognizes abuse and involvement in the treatment program.

- Shows commitment to recovery.

- Shows progress towards achievement of goals and areas of employment.

- Shows ongoing sobriety.

- Addresses entry issues as part of a better life goal plan.

- Understands why vocational rehabilitation is needed.

- Addresses entry issues as part of a better life call.

- Understands why vocational rehabilitation is an effective program for maintaining sobriety.

- Is able to independently complete process keeping a job.

Vocational Rehabilitation Services

- *Referral* - Clients can be self-referred or referred by the rehabilitation institution, family, or physicians.

- *Application* - The vocational rehabilitation service counselor gathers and evaluates information to determine work eligibility. This involves an assessment of the physical and/or mental impairment.

- *Extended evaluation* - When additional information is needed to determine work eligibility, the counselor may need additional time to determine disability and possibilities.

Rehabilitation Program Development

The counselor and client must both determine a job that will allow the client to reach certain goals. The job goal and other objectives are specified in an Individualized Plan for Employment (IPE). Services may include:

- Vocational guidance and counseling

- Mental health treatment to correct or modify an impairment

- Training (vocational school or on-the-job)

- Rehabilitation technology (assistive devices)

- Placement assistance and follow-up

Vocational and Habilitation Options

- *Supported Employment (SE) -* This involves a situation where persons with severe disabilities are placed in positions with qualified job coaches who provide ongoing support services so the client can retain employment.

- *Independent Living Services (ILS) -* These services promote independent living, including client control, self-help, peer support, equal access, and system advocacy. These things are done to maximize the integration and inclusion of the person into the community with independence and productivity.

In group counseling, the counselor describes, selects, and appropriately uses strategies from accepted and culturally appropriate models.

The Attributes of a Group Counselor

Knowledge

Group counselors should be knowledgeable of a variety of group methods appropriate to achieving client objectives in a treatment population, including methods in group problem solving, decision-making, and addressing group conflict. Counselors must understand the leadership, facilitator and counseling methods appropriate for each type of group and setting. A group counselor must be aware of and understand the criteria for screening and choosing group members, and the applicable age, gender, and culture-specific treatment strategies.

Counselors must have knowledge of the developmental processes that affect groups over time, or the stages of group development and appropriate counseling methods. These include the general principles for selecting group goals, outcomes and ground rules, as well as the principles for graduating members and ending groups. Counselors must also be prepared for those specific challenges and issues that arise with the addition or departure of a group member, both of which impact individuals and the group as a whole.

It is important for counselors to differentiate between the therapeutic and harmful uses of humor and can encourage the general characteristics of therapeutic group behavior, discouraging negative behavior. Similarly, counselors must be aware of the types of power in the therapeutic group process and the use of authority in that process.

Overall, group counselors must understand the definitions of process and content and distinguish between the group process and the content of discussion. More specifically, group counselors should have a deep understanding of how process variables affect the ability of the group to focus on content and how content affects the ability of the group to focus on process.

Finally, group counselors must be current on research concerning the effectiveness of varying models and strategies for group counseling with general populations, populations with substance use disorders, and members of varying cultural groups.

Skills

Counselors must adapt group counseling skills as appropriate for the type of group. Counselors must be adept at designing and instilling group-specific therapeutic strategies. Counseling skills include methods that stimulate progress toward both individual and group goals and documenting that progress. Methods should align with both process and content. A skilled group counselor uses group process to determine group goals, outcomes, and ground rules, so that these objectives remain nestled in the individual context of the group and its members. Counselors observe group process; furthermore, counselors must effectively handle resistance, transference, and countertransference and also determine when appropriate to intervene in group process.

The group process helps a counselor determine the appropriate criteria and methods for a client's transition to the next appropriate level of care; in this way, counselors can use group process to prepare group members for transition and to resolve transitional issues. Counselors must be able to recognize when members are ready to exit.

Despite the group atmosphere, counselors need to recognize individual needs. This begins with assessing whether an individual client is appropriate for participation in the group at all. Counselors may need to redesign individual treatment plans following observation of clients in group settings, documenting that behavior in group that may have implications for treatment planning. However, counselors must keep in mind that while a client's behavior in group can be reflective of his or her treatment needs, it not always is. Overall, counselors must be aware of the similarities and differences between the needs of individuals and group processes even while accommodating and recognizing individual needs within the group as appropriate.

While there is a place for humor in group counseling, the counselor should use it appropriately.

Attitudes

Group counselors should always be non-judgmental.

Group counselors must maintain an attitude of respect for group members at all times. It is imperative that group members be involved in setting collective rules, goals, and determinants of termination and graduation, and that the counselor recognize this collaborative atmosphere. Counselors should also be mindful of the role of group members in the group process, balancing that with taking steps toward intervention as appropriate. Counselors must be respectful of different views and experiences of group members, especially keeping in mind the differences in rates of progression towards treatment goals between different group members. Additionally, group counselors should remain mindful of the emotional impact of the entry and exit of group members on others in the group.

Flexibility is a key component of group counseling. Counselors should remain flexible regarding the diverse counseling strategies to accommodate the differing needs of group members as well as the group as a whole.

Counseling for Families, Couples, and Significant Others

An understanding of families, couples, and significant others affected by substance use and their relationships with the addict is key for counselors.

Knowledge

Counselors working with families and significant others of addicts, and with couples, need a strong understanding of the impact substance abuse, dependence, and use has on family relationships, and alternately, how those relationships impact substance use and abuse. Furthermore, the counselor must understand how the behaviors resulting from substance abuse impact family relationships (and vice versa).

In working with an addict's family and/or social system, counselors should have a strong knowledge of the assessment tools used with addicts' families and significant others. Counselors must be knowledgeable of intervention techniques applicable to different problems at different stages of development and recovery.

To help families, couples, and significant others achieve recovery-oriented goals from a systems perspective, counselors need a knowledge of the counseling strategies associated with recovery and of healthy behavioral patterns in family and social systems.

Working with families and significant others of addicts includes understanding how a family's culture and/or religious background impacts their understanding of substance abuse; cultural sensitivity can make planning an intervention more effective.

Domestic violence is a feature in many addicts' families. Counselors must be able to recognize the signs of domestic violence and patterns of abuse. Counselors need a strong knowledge of the law regarding domestic violence and violence against

53

persons; furthermore, they must be able to provide victims with appropriate resources. Finally, counselors must be able to develop intervention strategies not only for addicts in active addition, but also for victims of violence.

Often, the addict is not ready or willing to confront his or her addiction. The counselor must be able to help the addict's family or significant others focus on their own issues and emotional recovery even if the addict is unwilling to join counseling. Likewise, counselors need a firm grasp of the stages of recovery not only for addicts, but for their families and loved ones as well.

Counselors should know about confidentiality regulations and how to effectively and appropriately apply them.

Finally, counselors for families, couples, and significant others of addicts should be knowledgeable about current research and literature on systems theory and dynamics. They should remain current on research and literature examining interventions related to substance abuse, including that which involves violence.

Skills

An effective addiction counselor for families, couples, and significant others must demonstrate mastery of several skills. Counselors must effectively apply appropriate assessment tools. Counselors must always respect confidentiality regulations.

Counselors should help families and significant others identify goals based on the concerns of individual members as well as concerns of the social system. Furthermore, the addiction counselor should be able to choose the appropriate intervention with the family member or other system member in order to move toward the set treatment goals.

Counselors must be able to understand the role each individual plays in the family or social system of the addict, as well as those dynamics that could affect recovery. Furthermore, they must be able to constructively explain harmful dynamics to addicts' families and significant others, educating them on how to spot and stop those patterns and identify and practice more beneficial ones, in both the immediate and long term.

Developing constructive, helpful patterns of social and familial interaction with members of the family and social system includes teaching them to resolve negative situations caused by the addict due to substance-induced behavior or behavioral changes.

Counselors should be sensitive to cultural perspectives on family relationships and substance abuse. Cultural sensitivity applies to developing goals and developing intervention strategies.

Attitudes

At all times, counselors working with members of addicts' social systems should maintain an attitude of respect for members of those systems while seeing the system as a whole as a client itself. It follows that counselors should recognize the complexity of counseling families, couples, and significant others. As such, counselors should remain flexible and open to the variety of approaches to counseling these social systems. Counselors should be aware and respectful of cultural influences that affect the dynamics, interactions, and relationships within a family or social system.

Not all members of family and social systems are prepared for participation in counseling; therefore, counselors should especially appreciate the benefit of collaboration with individuals ready and eager to participate. Meanwhile, counselors should be mindful of the needs and concerns of other systems members in helping them understand the relationship between the social system and substance abuse behavior, including ongoing family and social dynamics. Understand and frame destructive behaviors of the family and significant others as systemic issues.

Counselors should always be mindful of confidentiality and applicable regulations.

Health Issues

User training, knowledge, and skills regarding STDs help educate the recovering addict regarding transmission. To apply this in a group or one-on-one setting, the counselor will need to gain experience. In some cases, counselors train alongside mentors and work to apply theory to real-world settings. This includes:

- Recognize all physical signs of STDs that can occur with a patient. This can include lesions on the skin, bruising, fevers, persistent coldness, and other similar attributes.

- Provide the group with education on the risk of infection.

- Instruct on ways the person could prevent transmission to another individual.

- Offer appropriate coping skills to the group during this experiment.

- Explain treatment methods that are used for different types of STDs.

- Determine display of risky behavior that is present within the group.

Experiential Therapy

Experiential therapy uses role play, guided imagery, props, and other activities to help clients explore subconscious feelings, anxieties, and other issues, emphasizing personal responsibility. There is no one specific type of therapy: in addition to the examples listed, experiential therapy may include music, art, wilderness, equine, recreation, and adventure therapy. Experiential therapy also allows clients to explore personal relationships and their behavior. In terms of substance abuse, addicts can learn which feelings or situations trigger compulsions or harmful behaviors; recreating these triggering situations help the client address difficult feelings and learn to manage them.

Emotions are a direct reflection of a person's personal reality. They tell the individual's story of his or her life, regardless of how good or bad that may be. This helps participants locate and decipher emotions that have been stored away. Clients can experience negative episodes from the past, and this allows them to identify the emotions related to those episodes. Once this occurs, the client can create solutions to resolve the damage and promote self-healing.

Examples of Experiential Therapy

- Psychodrama
- Recreation therapy
- Music therapy
- Equine therapy
- Adventure therapy
- Wilderness therapy
- Expressive art therapy

Benefits of Experiential Therapy

There are numerous benefits and advantages of experiential therapy. These include:

- Provides opportunities for the counselor to observe the client in situations where the client is not focused on the therapy.

- Allows recovery under the supervision of a qualified, skilled therapist.

- Develops improved self-esteem.

- Allows the recovering addict to take responsibility for his or her actions.

- Is a personal empowerment and emotional growth experience.

Family and Addiction

Overview of Family and Addiction Issues

The recovering addict's family plays an important role in both the active addiction and recovery process. According to addiction experts, these people may take part in the use, abuse, or overuse of substances and enable the patient to continue using. There are two functions in family addiction:

- Primary causes and issues with the patient's well-being, functioning, and level of recovery.

- Therapy to resolve family issues from the past and to determine how abuse affects each member in the family.

The benefits of therapy include creating change within the family structure, developing techniques to improve family functioning, strengthening and supporting family members, and teaching coping skills to family members.

Types of Families

- *Functional* – The family system is stable and the user is typically in the early stages of addiction.

- *Neurotic enmeshed* – Abuse is considered a symptom/cause of the family dynamics/dysfunction. Communication is poor, and fighting is common.

- *Disintegrated* – There is some temporary separation between the substance user and the family members. This is when a neurotic enmeshed family progresses to a later stage of the addiction.

- *Absent* – With this family type, there is permanent separation between the addict and the members of the family.

Counseling Techniques

- *Joining:* The ability to connect, understand, and build strength within families. This is stabilized by helping the patient stop abuse by creating goals within the family. This helps the recovering addict see how his or her behavior change affects the family.

- *Education:* Addiction and resources are provided to the patient and family members. In addition, the recovering addict can utilize outside resources in order to continue on a successful recovery path.

- *Structured analysis:* Determine reasons why a family does not work, examine problems, and figure out a solution for better family dynamics.

- *Alternative coping techniques:* Teach honest demonstration of feelings to family members so that they can express their emotions and determine how they can use them to solve problems.

- *Relapse prevention:* Plan to prevent and cope in the event of a relapse; this can include the family's ability to prevent relapse.

- *Drug substitution:* This is the substitution of a legal drug for an illegal one to assist the patient in making positive changes. An example of this would be a methadone program.

Verbal, physical, and psychological abuse all are used by family members against each other. Many studies have shown that violence and addiction go hand-in-hand - over one-half of men convicted of battery have addiction problems.

The actual use of drugs and alcohol has not been established as the *cause* of the abuse—rather, abuse is a learned technique. Violence is used to control the victim. Many women who are subjected to abuse use drugs in order to cope with the abuse. Additionally, they may seek partners who have addiction problems of their own. Counselors must determine the dynamics that surround use and abuse by family members.

Domestic Violence Diagnosis and Assessment

Women are convicted every year of domestic violence offenses, but it is more common for men to be the abuser in a heterosexual relationship. During the process of treatment, the counselor must interview both the victim and abuser in order to gain a complete understanding of the abuse present within the relationship. Diagnosis and assessment of domestic violence involves:

- Discovering family dynamics revolving around addiction and abuse.

- Identifying issues within the family in order to evaluate and treat them.

- Examining each person's beliefs regarding family issues.

Three Common Myths about Battering

- *Myth: Battering is a disease.*
  Truth: The batterer abuses because he or she suffers from low self-esteem.

- *Myth: Loss of emotion is a direct cause of battering.*
  Truth: Abusers know it is wrong, but they batter in order to feel better about themselves.

- *Myth: Battering occurs due to lack of self-control.*
  Truth: Abuse is a learned behavior, and many times, the person abusing will have suffered abuse in the past, now using it to gain control.

Techniques Used for Domestic Violence Treatment

While the techniques used for domestic violence treatment vary based on each unique case, there are a variety of techniques used within domestic violence cases that have proven effective. These techniques are used to address the issue of abuse, examine how it relates to the addiction, and determine steps to stop the abuse from occurring in the future. Some of the most effective techniques include:

- *Funneling* - This is a process to determine how each person within the relationship views abuse, done during individual or couples sessions. This information is generally revealed over time in small pieces.

- *Interviewing* - The counselor must interview each member of the family separately in order to allow each person to speak freely about their feelings regarding different issues of abuse and addiction.

- *Emotional expression* - Ask both partners to specify if they feel that the abuse is justified, and if so, why? This allows the counselor to examine underlying issues within the patient that may be difficult to see on the surface, such as low self-esteem in a patient who makes excuses for their abusive partner.

- *Be assertive* - The counselor must be direct with a questioning process for the patient, the abuser, or the victim during the time of the questioning.

- *Detect* – Determine if the abuser or victim is making excuses, and address and explore these excuses.

- *Eliminate blaming* - Stop blaming the use of a substance for the cause of the battery.

- *Provide education* - Educate both the abuser and victim on substance abuse, and how it is not the cause of battering.

- *Analyze level of abuse* - The counselor must take the proper steps in order to protect the patient from serious, impending harm.

- *Incorporate proper therapy sessions* - Work with patients alone and together in order to develop a nonviolence plan. If patient is the abuser, the counselor must help them create a non-violence plan in order to stop him or her from becoming violent during times of aggression.

- *Examine different areas* - Examine all aspects of the abuse in terms of the feelings that are associated, the amount and when it occurs.

- *Determine results* - Determine how substance abuse plays a role in couple dynamics. For example, does substance abuse occur during the time of battery, prior to, or after? While getting answers to these questions, examine and address feelings associated with violence.

- *Monitor behavior* - Examine behavioral changes within the patient during the time of the interview, and develop appropriate coping strategies to change the behaviors.

- *Provide resources* - Refer the patient to self-help groups, as this will help them to cope with the abuse by developing peers, support, and coping skills. These things help them to modify and change the behavior on a long-term basis.

Three Stages in the Cycle of Abuse

1. *Increased tension* - An increase in the amount of tension that occurs within the household.

2. *Violence* – The situation becomes violent in the form of physical or psychological abuse.

3. *Compensation* - The abuser may become apologetic. Once forgiven, or forgotten, the cycle will almost always start back at stage one. It's important to teach the victim this cycle and how to watch for increased tension again.

Research has proven that the main risk periods for drug abuse are during major transitions in the life of the adolescent. The first major transition is leaving a secure environment (such as middle or high school), and entering another school. This is when adolescents are likely to encounter drugs for the first time. Adolescents face many emotional, social, and educational challenges during high school, so there is more exposure and availability of drugs. A greater risk occurs when young adults leave home to attend college or work on their own for the first time.

During the last 20 years, researchers have attempted to determine how drug use begins during adolescence and how it progresses. Several risk factors add to a person's propensity for substance abuse, but protective factors reduce it.

Risk Factors

- Low parental supervision

- Limited communication with parents

- Conflict or frequent confrontation in the family or home

- Lack of discipline

- Severe discipline

- Inconsistent discipline

- History of drug or alcohol abuse among family members

- Sexual abuse

- Thrill-seeking behaviors

- Emotional instability

- Learning or emotional challenges or disabilities

- Inability to cope in social situations

- Affiliations with peers who use alcohol or drugs, or who engage in deviant behaviors

Protective Factors

- Strong, positive familial connections

- Parental monitoring and engagement in teen activities

- Parental involvement

- Successful performance in school

- Strong bond with religious organization

- Clear, enforceable rules of conduct

Testing Methods

A counselor may administer tests to determine an adolescent's propensity for substance abuse or current level of substance abuse.

Professional Experience Questionnaire

- Forty-question testing process.

- Fourth-grade level of education testing

- Examines levels of addiction severity

- Examines psychological and behavioral issues involved in the addiction process

- Examines personal and environmental issues

- Determines age and the frequency of substance use

SaSSI Testing

- Distinguishes between use and abuse

- Age test used for persons aged twelve years and older

- Seventy-question testing process

- Used to determine types of treatment available

- Present with or without psychological issues

Counseling Adolescents

The way that addiction affects the adolescent can vary based on different aspects regarding the child, such as his or her temperament, or the level of negative occurrences that result within the family due to the addiction. In order to determine how the addiction is affecting the child, the following steps should be taken:

- Ask how the family member's addiction affects the adolescent.

- Determine how both the adolescent and the user may play a role within the addiction process. It is important to assure the adolescent that he or she is not responsible for the addiction, but that they can take measures to ensure they are not enabling a family member who is abusing drugs or alcohol.

- Create a positive and effective plan based on the effects the addiction has on the adolescent and family.

- Develop a recovery plan based on the level of impact of the addiction on the family and the resultant social and emotional problems.

- Determine if the problem faced is the real issue within the family, or if denial of the addiction is the real factor. A continued denial of the addiction will lead to long-term negative effects for the entire family, and this could result in death due to overdose from unintentional enabling by the family.

- When denial of addiction is present, the family must first learn to accept the addiction as a real issue before it can be properly addressed.

Assessment of Substance Abuse, Lethality, and Level of Care

An individual arrives at treatment for substance abuse in one of several ways. An addict may be sent to treatment by court order, as a condition of probation or parole, as the result of an intervention, or as a result of self-identification (voluntarily). In these cases screening and assessments to determine if the individual has a problem with substance abuse play an important role; these techniques also play a role in designing interventions.

When taking an assessment, the counselor collects data about the client and other sources to gauge the severity of the individual's addiction. During the assessment, the counselor also determines what support the individual needs and what his or her weaknesses and assets are. This data is necessary to develop a treatment plan with strategic goals, plans to achieve those goals, and appropriate resources. A thorough assessment is imperative in order to stabilize the client and prevent the development or worsening of any serious health issues with potentially fatal consequences.

Rehabilitation and Treatment Programs

While there are many kinds of treatment programs and rehabilitation settings, caring for the recovering addict is always the central focus. Depending on the severity of the addiction as determined through the assessment process and diagnosis, programs could consist of anything from education to a comprehensive residential inpatient program. Any treatment should be patient-centered and individualized.

Treatment follows a continuum of services: facilities coordinate programming with appropriate partners such as medical and community resources. Treatment should allow addicts to develop in recovery, progressing along the continuum toward positive treatment outcomes and goals.

In treatment and rehabilitation, case management coordinates patient care as clients progress through the continuum of treatment. Case managers should ensure that clients receive individual, group and family counseling as part of their recovery. Furthermore, case managers and treatment programs should ensure that special populations such as those with dual diagnoses, those living with HIV/AIDS, the homeless, the elderly, LGBT, ethnic and racial minorities, and both females and males are treated with their specific needs in mind.

Relapse Prevention

Helping prevent relapse is an essential part of any treatment program, and it starts with analyzing what triggers a client to use or behave problematically. Clients must learn to make choices and decisions to avoid relapse rather than facilitate it; they learn to avoid those triggers and, when they do encounter them, they must learn to handle situations and emotions more constructively.

Discuss the abstinence violation effect (AVE) with your client. AVE is a phenomenon wherein an addict believes abstinence is too difficult, and abuses substances as a result. When the addict attempts to refrain from this negative behavior (drug abuse) and fails in the attempt, he or she feels conflicted, guilt and/or shame as a result of the behavior, and uses more as a means to cope with those negative feelings, triggering continued drug use and associated harmful behavior.

Substance Abuse and Pre-Adolescents

Children who are part of a household with addiction suffer from lack of trust, no sense of self-worth, boundary issues, lack of feelings, impulsivity, self-harm and other negative feelings that they project on themselves or to others. These children may also experience a feeling of guilt for the person who is abusing drugs or alcohol, which may encourage additional use.

Experiential Practicum

Recovering addicts, domestic abusers, and victims of abuse must create their own definition of domestic abuse and identify different keywords associated with it. In doing so, they come to understand how they relate to abuse and determine thought patterns that could have a negative impact on the person being treated. While completing this process, the client should:

- Determine how he or she learned to define domestic abuse, such as through television or other media.

- Identify how he or she associates with the terms linked with addiction recovery and abuse.

- After the person has analyzed feelings associated with these terms, he or she can use the definitions in both a negative and positive manner. For negative thoughts regarding different areas of domestic abuse, he or she can recognize these thoughts, learn more about that area of abuse, and then take steps to change thought patterns in a way that will not affect the patient.

- Once the person has positive definitions of certain areas involving domestic violence, such as recovering from violence, the person can use these terms during certain times. While technical terms may be difficult for some people to understand, some can allow the patient to develop an understanding regarding certain areas of their abuse and/or addiction.

- Definitions can be used during both group and individual counseling.

Spirituality, Change and Motivation

Spirituality

It is crucial that discussions of spirituality proceed at the patient's pace and volition. A counselor may ask about faith traditions or spirituality, but should not press a patient who is not inclined to discuss it. However, if the patient is willing to discuss religion and spirituality, a counselor may find important components of the addiction and recovery process in the patient's individual beliefs.

Patients suffering from addiction commonly have little or no spirituality. Many times, when addiction has become prolonged, negative, and life changing, the patient can experience a disconnection from themselves and their prior beliefs – or may never have had any to begin with. The patient may also experience a feeling of indifference to the topic of spirituality, or have a hard time connecting with his or her beliefs. One of the most common cases of feeling indifferent to spirituality is due to misunderstanding. Many patients are not familiar with the difference between spirituality and religion, and can mistake them for one concept. When this is the case, certain ideas associated with particular faith traditions can cause indifference or hostility to any concept associated with either religion or spirituality.

The inability to connect with the spiritual self, lack of understanding, and other issues involving this area could lead to difficulties with the patient's spirituality, or a complete lack of spiritual presence. Many studies regarding spirituality have found that this lack can affect the addiction process greatly, because some individuals have a difficult time with recovery if they do not connect with their spirituality.

Issues of Spirituality in Recovery

Some issues seen within recovery regarding spirituality include:

- Lack of any type of spirituality within their lives
- Lack of understanding of how religion is different from spirituality

Spirituality is a component of many addiction treatment programs as part of overall therapy. Issues regarding spirituality are sometimes vitally important to a patient's recovery. The process of treatment based in spirituality is often seen to have similar characteristics as a Twelve Step program. When discussing spirituality with a patient, remember the following:

- Never push spiritual beliefs on to a patient. There is nothing wrong with a patient choosing atheism or agnosticism.
- Refer the patient to spiritual groups only if he or she wishes.

Many problems of mind, body and spirit spring from addiction – so as the patient undergoes the recovery process, the counselor can help them develop a solid recovery plan based on their individual physical, mental and spiritual characteristics.

A reminder: It is not only unethical for a counselor to push spirituality onto a patient, but can be harmful and counterproductive, instantly destroying carefully constructed trust and positive relationship dynamics. However, during the initial assessment of the patient, and in order to determine what the patient's feelings toward spirituality are, the counselor can assess this aspect of recovery with the consent of the patient.

Addiction experts who study the results of change within patients have discovered that the use of motivational counseling techniques is one of the most effective therapies. Change and motivational counseling can provide lifelong recovery for those affected by addiction.

Change in the Addict

Changes occur when the patient:

- Makes a connection between his or her life problems and the process of addiction.

- Develops an action plan for use throughout recovery.

- Takes part in interconnected change and self-discovery.

- Develops positive attitudes and maintains them throughout recovery.

- Maintains hope throughout the recovery process with positive coping skills.

- Continues to keep perspective, even during difficult times.

Stages of Change

1. *Pre-contemplation* - The patient is not looking for change, and the addiction doesn't seem to be an issue. He or she usually starts to recognize that addiction is present during the pre-contemplation stage.

2. *Preparation* - The patient plans to make a change, but may have failed in the past, or may have created a plan and failed to actively participate in it. Small, insignificant changes are made by the patient during the preparation stage.

3. *Action* - During this stage, a commitment to change is made. The patient works with the counselor in order to determine different areas of their life that need to be modified, such as behavior and environmental exposure.

4. *Maintenance:* During this stage, changes are maintained for six months or longer.

5. *Termination:* During the fifth stage, major changes are made. Relaxation is no longer an issue for the patient, as he or she continues to be active in recovery. Although termination of the addiction can be achieved with the right mindset, complete termination is difficult to reach, because addiction is often a life-long, ongoing process of change that needs constant maintenance.

The Benefits of Motivational Counseling

- It helps the patient to engage in an early treatment plan.

- It is useful when the patient shows resistance to change during the process of treatment with the counselor.

The Phases of Motivational Counseling

- *Empathy* - During this phase, the counselor positively accepts the patient, creates a comfortable environment, acts with genuine concern and kindness, and focuses on learning about the patient and his or her prior history (not only with abuse, but in other areas of life that have affected well-being). The empathy process invites and allows for permanent change.

- *Discrepancy* - Often paired with self-sufficient and empathetic processes. It helps the patient to determine what areas need to be addressed. The counselor will work with the patient in order to help him or her develop love and trust in the self. This can be done by developing external and internal support. Discrepancy helps the patient to see that change is possible, and helps the patient become less likely to rationalize or project areas of change.

- *Resistance* - Preventative steps are taken by the counselor to help avoid power struggle during this stage. The spirit of motivational counseling must be present during all sessions in order for this therapy to be effective and for the recovery process to be successful.

All human beings are individuals who are shaped by a confluence of environmental, individual, experiential and cultural factors. There are no "silver bullet" treatment plans for all white males any more than there are one-size-fits-all treatment plans for black women. Every individual is different, and stereotypes do not serve a counselor's quest to help a patient in their recovery process. However, it is important for the counselor to be aware of elements commonly found in cultures, mores, norms, relational statuses to majority populations and societal expectations within specific populations.

Gender-appropriate and culturally responsive counseling improves long-term outcomes for patients. The risks of substance abuse differ by race, gender, sexual orientation, age, ethnicity, and other factors. These disorders also involve education, economic status, geographic location, and culture. Understanding special populations is critical for implementing an effective substance abuse therapy plan.

Latino/Latina

There are around forty million Latino/Latina people in the U.S. The socioeconomic status of many members of this population reflects circumstances of recent immigration or being the first natural born citizen in a family of immigrants. In a recent survey of Hispanic/Latino men and women, thirty-three percent of men and twelve percent of women admitted to heavy drinking. The main substances used among Hispanic people are opiates and crack/cocaine.

Treatment programs for Latinos and Latinas sometimes focus on developing services that endorse culturally competent practices and create an environment that honors their heritage and incorporates certain appropriate cultural values. Substance abuse counseling based on a family model is often effective. Additionally, gender roles are often important, with emphasis on aspects of "marianisimo" and "machismo" such as strength, flexibility, and the ability to survive.

African-American

This highest population density of African Americans is in Southern states and in cities around the country. The largest racial minority in America, at 12.1% of the population, many black people experience legacy poverty resulting from centuries of institutionalized racism and still suffer its lasting socioeconomic effects; these include difficulty accessing quality education, being unfairly treated in regards to employment, and trouble securing housing outside of high-crime, low-property-value neighborhoods. Substance use among this special population has been in decline since the 1990s, though recent studies indicate that alcohol use accounts for around twenty-five percent of treatment admissions for African American women. Around thirty-five percent of admissions to treatment facilities for African Americans in general are for cocaine abuse.

It is necessary for African Americans to have access to services that provide adequate social support during addiction recovery. They often are at risk for substance use due to exposure to economic stressors and biopsychosocial issues that lead to coping difficulties and emotional distress. From a racial standpoint, African Americans bear a disproportionate burden of heterosexual HIV infection, a fact the counselor should bring up any time a black patient admits to drug use by injection. Effective treatments include social networks, family therapy, and community involvement.

Asian and Pacific American

Asian origins include countries such as India, China, Cambodia, Japan, Korea, Vietnam, and the Philippines. More than seven million Asian and Pacific Americans live in America. This group represents one percent of admissions to substance abuse treatment centers, but this number has increased in the last decade. As many Asian-Americans lacking a genetic enzyme that breaks down alcohol, they often are especially vulnerable to alcohol intoxication and much more severe aftereffects than many other racial populations. Thus, Asian-Americans have the lowest percentage of current alcohol problems or histories of alcohol abuse. The rates of illicit drug use are also low among Asian and Pacific Americans. According to recent data, methamphetamine is the drug most often used by this group.

Treatment is often effective when it involves the family, as many Asian and Pacific-American cultures have values that place greater importance on the influence of extended family members. Acculturation stress and its relationship to substance use should be assessed in recent immigrants. The women of this special population often assume the role of the primary caretaker, and sometimes bear a disproportionate amount of the work of supporting and nurturing children.

Assessment, Clinical Evaluation, Treatment Planning, Family and Community Education and Case Management
(70 hours)

Assessment of Substance Abuse, Lethality, and Levels of Care

To successfully assess, diagnose, manage, and treat an addict, it is imperative that a counselor fully comprehend the extent of a client's addiction and how it affects other areas of his or her life. During the assessment and screening, the counselor should start to develop this understanding and an individualized, appropriate treatment plan. Gathering the correct information is essential in order to develop a suitable treatment plan; therefore, during the initial interview with the client, counselors must follow protocols. Counselors must also use standardized assessment and screening tools.

Six Areas of Assessment

1. Determine client behaviors, values, and frequency of use.

2. Identify why substance use is a problem.

3. Determine how that patient's life is affected by the substance use.

4. Identify the location, timeframe, and method of treatment.

5. Recognize any reinforcement for change needed by the patient.

6. Examine factors specific to culture and spirituality-related issues.

How Screening and Assessment Differ

During screening, a counselor determines the following: whether a problem is present, the nature and severity of the problem, and a proper diagnosis. In short, counselors use screening to determine whether a substance user requires assessment. During an assessment, the counselor obtains more detailed information about the client and his or her circumstances in order to design a treatment plan tailored to his or her needs.

Factors that Influence Screening and Assessment

Culture and Ethnicity

As has been discussed throughout the text, counselors must be mindful of the specific cultural background of the client. Depending on a client's cultural background, he or she may be troubled by the processes of screening and assessment, finding them intrusive or even threatening. In addition, differing concepts of mental health may confuse some clients: they may not have experience with counseling or understand its purpose. Furthermore, counselors should keep in mind that clients may have had poor experiences with social service workers or programs in the past and so be distrustful of encounters with counselors and treatment programs. Counselors must be sensitive to the backgrounds and experiences of these clients and willing to learn about their cultures, beliefs, behaviors and attitudes as part of developing tailored treatment plans. Some strategies follow:

- Instruments and tools should adapted for people of specific cultural groups and populations.

- Interviews conducted in the client's language by a trained staff member.

- Thorough discussion to facilitate full understanding of substance use.

Socioeconomic Status

Counselors should be aware of the expectations as they are based on socioeconomic status. Perceptions could lead to failures to detect drug use in certain patient populations. For instance, healthcare providers often forget to ask middle to upper level income patients about substance use.

Substance Abuse Screening Tools

The objective of substance abuse screening is to identify persons likely to have alcohol or drug use problems. Screening is often conducted by an interview or a short, written questionnaire. Self-administered tools are more likely than face-to-face interviews to elicit honest answers, especially regarding the use of drugs and alcohol. Tools include:

- *The Alcohol Use Disorder Identification Test (AUDIT)* - This is a widely used screening tool effective for identifying heavy drinking. It is a ten-question, self-administered test.

- *The Texas Christian University Drug Screen II (TCUDS II)* - This is a fifteen-item, self-administered substance abuse test that takes around ten minutes to complete. It is widely used in the criminal justice setting.

- *CAGE-AID - The CAGE and CAGE-AID* are questionnaires involving simple tests that screen drug and alcohol consumption.

- *Mini-International Neuropsychiatric Interview (MINI)* - This is a brief, structured interview used for major substance use disorders. It takes around thirty minutes.

Substance Use Assessment

The assessment of a client's life examines details for accurate diagnosis and an appropriate therapy plan and treatment goals. Qualified and trained counselors will perform a comprehensive assessment to determine these things. The assessment should involve multiple avenues to obtain the needed clinical information, such as clinical records, structured interviews, assessment measures, and collateral information. Assessment is a fluid process that continues throughout treatment. Periodic reassessment is necessary for determining client progress and changing therapy needs.

The Assessment Interview

The counselor has to conduct a clinical assessment interview, which requires sensitivity and a considerable amount of time. This is the start of the therapeutic relationship for the client and the counselor. The interviewer should initially explain the reason for the psychosocial history. In addition, the counselor needs to make appropriate referrals within and outside the facility during this time. During the interview, the counselor should:

- Determine the goals of the assessment process.

- Decide what resources are needed to administer and score the assessment instrument, interpret the results, and establish appropriate services.

- Decide what screening measures are required for this client.

- Use a standardized formal assessment tool that offers uniformity and consistency.

The Psychosocial History

This part of the assessment includes:

- *Medical History and Physical Health*: While it is important to review any medical conditions with a client during an assessment, counselors should especially discuss those conditions for which substance abusers are at high risk, including a client's HIV/AIDS status and risk behavior; history of infectious diseases like hepatitis C; history of sexually transmitted diseases; use of hormone replacement therapy; use of birth control; the relationship between gynecological problems and substance abuse; history of pregnancies, abortions, miscarriages, and substance abuse during pregnancy; and any need for prenatal care.

- *Substance Abuse History*: Counselors should review the ways and reasons clients began using drugs and continued to abuse substances. Counselors should also review any history of substance abuse in the client's family of origin and in current or previous significant relationships. Finally, counselors should explore the client's history of substance use with members of his or her family and/or significant others.

- *Mental Health and Treatment History*: Counselors should discuss any history of previous treatment and the nature of the client's relationship with those providers, as well as the consequences of treatment. Counselors should discuss any diagnoses of anxiety or mood disorders with the client, any history of traumatic events and PTSD, and eating disorders. In addition, counselors must determine the severity of any threats to the safety of the client and/or others, including suicidal ideation and para-suicidal behaviors, threats of suicide, and history of violence and abuse (including sexual violence and abuse). The counselor should also discuss any history of mental illness in the client's family of origin. Discuss the client's personal strengths and history of coping strategies here.

- *Interpersonal and Family History*: Determine the extent of substance abuse in the client's current significant relationship (if any). Discuss the level of acceptance of the client's addiction in his or her family and among his or her significant relationships, and any support received from them in receiving treatment. Finally, review any child care needs with the client.

- *Family, Parenting, and Caregiver History*: If applicable, discuss any parenting or caregiver roles the client has held in the past or present.

- *Children's Developmental and Educational History* (applicable to women and

78

children programs): Here, the counselor should assess any child safety needs. The counselor should also determine the child/children's medical, developmental, or emotional needs, if any.

- *Sociocultural History*: Counselors must assess the client's social support system, including isolation before treatment and support for recovery. Review the client's culture, including attitudes toward substance abuse and recovery, especially beliefs and taboos relating to women and substance abuse. Furthermore, counselors should explore any cultural conflicts or stressors the client is currently experiencing or has experienced in the past. Determine the need for bilingual services or services in other languages. Finally, discuss the client's current spiritual beliefs and practices (if any).

- *Vocational, Educational, and Military History*: Determine if the client is employed and if he or she is supported in recovery by the employer. Likewise, assess the client's military history (if any), including history of traumatic events during military service and any substance abuse during that time. Finally, determine whether the client is financially independent and to what extent.

- *Legal History*: Assess the client's history of involvement and current relationship with child protective services, if any, as well as custody disputes. Gather details regarding the client's arrest record, history of incarceration, and history of restraining orders, if any. In the case of single parents (generally women), ascertain their history of child placement during periods of incarceration (past and present).

- *Barriers to Treatment and Related Services*: Assess the client's needs regarding child care, health insurance, transportation, finances, and case management. Review other potential barriers to treatment.

- *Strengths and Coping Strategies*: Review how the client has managed challenges in the past; review previous attempts at recovery and failed strategies; assess successful coping mechanisms practiced by the client in managing life challenges.

Assessment Tools for Substance Use Disorders

- *Addiction Severity Index (ASI)* - The most widely used assessment tool. It assesses seven domains of the client's life. The ASI-F expanded the ASI by accounting for familial, social, and psychiatric elements of a client's life experience.

- *Texas Christian University Brief Intake* - Used to assess drug, alcohol, psychological, legal, medical, and family aspects of the client's life.

- *Drinker Inventory of Consequences (DrinC)* - This tool is self-administered and assesses the negative consequences of drinking in five domains.

- *The Religious Practice and Beliefs Measurement* - A self-assessment tool that reviews religious practices and beliefs.

- *The Multidimensional Measure of Spirituality* - This assessment tool examines domains of spiritual activity, such as values and beliefs.

The clinical screening and assessment processes enable the counselor, the client, and the client's significant others to decide on the best course of action for recovery. These processes are an opportunity to tailor treatment to the individual circumstances and needs of the client, taking into account the available resources for treatment.

Clinical Screening

Screening establishes rapport and provides a framework for the management of crises, as well as determining the need for additional professional assistance.

Knowledge

In order to conduct a thorough and appropriate clinical screening, counselors must be aware of the purpose, importance, and methods of building a relationship with the client. Relationship-building requires a strong knowledge of the range of human emotions and feelings.

Counselors must develop a strong understanding of the client's mental status and presenting features, any psychiatric disorders, and the relationship of these conditions to the client's substance abuse. Counselors need a deep understanding of the effects of age, developmental level, culture, and gender on patterns and history of substance use, as well as how these variables affect client communication.

To carry out the screening process, counselors need expertise in validated screening instruments, including their purpose, application, and limitations. Counselors must gather data on a client's history of substance use and current use; current mental status; history of health, mental health, and substance-related treatment; and current environmental, social, and/or economic constraints. Counselors must also understand how to interpret the results of screening and how to gather and use information from collateral sources.

Furthermore, counselors require a knowledge of multi-axis diagnostic criteria and the current DSM or other accepted criteria for substance use disorders, including the strengths and limitations of such criteria. Counselors must also be aware of the use of commonly accepted criteria for client placement into levels of care.

Counselors must be knowledgeable about stages of readiness and stages of change models. They need a knowledge of the current validated instruments for assessing readiness to change. Counselors must be aware of and sensitive to the role of family and significant others in supporting or hindering change.

Counselors must have a knowledge of a broad range of treatment options. Counselors require a deep understanding of the continuum of care and the available range of treatment modalities. Furthermore, they will need to be familiar with the criteria for and determination of the appropriate content and format of the initial action plan.

Depending on the treatment plan, the patient may require referrals to varying facilities; thus, counselors need a strong knowledge of admissions and referral resources. In addition, counselors should be acutely aware of the protocols for admission and referral to treatment facilities and programs. Counselors should be aware of and adhere to the standards of ethics regarding referrals. At the same time, counselors need to keep client needs and preferences in mind. Finally, it is imperative that counselors have a strong knowledge of the proper documentation, confidentiality, and related procedures in referrals.

Substance abuse takes a tremendous toll on the human body and mind, and counselors should be mindful of the physical and psychological impact of substance abuse on the client. They should be knowledgeable and aware of the symptoms of intoxication, withdrawal, and toxicity for all psychoactive substances, both alone and in interaction with one another. They should particularly be familiar with the effects of chronic substance use or intoxication on cognitive abilities.

Counselors should be able to offer available resources for help with drug reactions, withdrawal, and violent behavior and know when to refer for toxicity screening or additional professional help. To this end, it is useful for a counselor to master the basic concepts of toxicity screening options, limitations, and legal implications, in addition to toxicology reporting language and the meaning of toxicology reports.

It is imperative that a counselor have a strong understanding of the relationship between psychoactive substance use and violence. This includes the basic diagnostic criteria for suicide risk, danger to others, withdrawal syndromes, and major psychiatric disorders. At the same time, counselors should be aware of mental and physical conditions that mimic drug intoxication, toxicity, and withdrawal. Finally, it is essential that counselors have some knowledge of the legal requirements concerning a client's potential for suicide and/or violent behavior.

Counselors should be able to identify what constitutes a crisis and understand the steps in crisis management. Counselors must also be able to identify situations in which additional professional assistance may be necessary and be aware of available sources of assistance.

In general, counselors should be knowledgeable of relevant policies and procedures, proper documentation, and appropriate application of confidentiality regulations.

Skills

Counselors must be able to accurately administer and score screening instruments and screen for physical and mental health status. It is key to obtain relevant information from the client; counselors must be skilled at gathering information and collecting appropriate data to make an accurate diagnosis and constructive recommendations. Furthermore, counselors should be able to determine relevant client characteristics, needs, and goals.

Communication is key for a counselor: counselors must communicate effectively and respectfully both verbally and non-verbally. Counselors must also communicate and document accurately and appropriately, writing accurately, concisely, and legibly.

Building a therapeutic relationship with a client includes identifying with the client's perspective and frame of reference. Counselors must respect and interpret the client's experiences. Counselors must display empathy, respect, and authenticity at all times. Understanding the client's feelings. Being respectful to the client in his or her state at the screening. Understanding how important it is for the counselor to display empathy when the client is expressing fear, anger, hopelessness, and/or suicidal or violent thoughts or feelings.

Counselors should be able to adopt a collaborative approach with the client to assess the impact of substance abuse on his or her life and the potential harmful effects of ongoing use. Counselors must gauge whether the client is ready to address his or her substance abuse problem, participate in treatment, and begin process of change. They must be able to apply accepted criteria for diagnosis of substance use disorders in making treatment recommendations. Upon such recommendations, counselors should be able to develop an initial action plan with the client and relevant significant others, accounting for the client's needs and available resources. Counselors must document the action plan and facilitate client follow-through. Finally, as part of the plan, counselors must have the ability to recommend appropriate treatment using proper placement criteria as applicable.

Properly developing a treatment plan and making recommendations includes recognition of one's own treatment biases and limitations. Counselors should understand and appreciate various treatment approaches and be willing to account for the client's best interest in making referrals and recommendations for treatment. To do so, counselors must network and advocate with service providers, negotiating and advocating client admissions to appropriate treatment resources.

Finally, all counselors must be able to handle crises effectively, recognizing dangerous situations and defusing them. A skilled counselor must quickly determine a client's potential for violence and/or suicide. Counselors are expected to intervene appropriately in situations when clients may be intoxicated.

Attitudes

Counselors must practice willingness during the screening process: a willingness to establish rapport with a client, to work in a collaborative way with clients and others, and to renegotiate plans. Counselors should be sensitive to clients' experiences and perspectives based on their race, cultural background, gender identity, sexual orientation, and other categories. It is essential that counselors value and appreciate the data gathering process.

Clinical Assessment

During the assessment, counselors work with the client and other stakeholders to collect and interpret more detailed information than that which is used in the screening. Assessment is a necessary, ongoing process to plan treatment and evaluate a client's progress. The counselor leads the client through a comprehensive assessment process that accounting for age, race, gender identity, cultural background, disabilities, and other factors. Some areas explored in the assessment process include the following:

- History of alcohol and other drug use
- Physical health, mental health, and addiction treatment history
- Psychological, emotional, and world-view concerns
- Current status of physical health, mental health, and substance use
- Family issues
- Work history and career issues
- History of criminality
- Spirituality
- Education and basic life skills

- Socio-economic characteristics and lifestyle

- Current legal status

- Use of community resources

- Knowledge

Counselors must be familiar with basic test validity and reliability, including the current validated assessment instruments and their subscales and the appropriate use and limitations of standardized instruments. Counselors must judge the range of life areas for assessment, taking into the account the influence of age, developmental level, racial and ethnic culture, gender, and disabilities on the validity and appropriateness of assessment instruments.

Knowledge

Counselors must understand the counselor's role, responsibilities, and scope of practice. At the same time, they must be aware of the limitations of their own training and education. As such, they should understand the supervisor's role. In addition, they should have a strong knowledge of available consultation services and roles of consultants as well as the range of available treatment options and agency-specific protocols and procedures.

Counselors should be deeply familiar with appropriate scoring methodology and strongly comfortable analyzing and interpreting results. At the same time, they should be aware of the multidisciplinary assessment approach.

Finally, counselors should be comfortable with appropriate terminology and abbreviations. They require a strong knowledge of the legal implications of actions and documentation and application of confidentiality regulations.

Skills

Counselors must be able to introduce the assessment and explain its purpose to the client. Counselors need to choose and administer those necessary assessment instruments that suit both the client and the counselor's scope of practice. Counselors need to explain instrument items and address client concerns while carrying out comprehensive interviews and gathering needed data from outside sources. Counselors are required to have a thorough understanding of scoring assessment tools and must be able to interpret the data that is relevant to the client. Part of correctly interpreting information is being able to utilize the results to identify appropriate treatment options; counselors need this skill.

Counselors must recognize and admit to their own limitations, including recognizing when consultation is appropriate and the need for assistance, including from a supervisor. That means taking that information into account during assessment findings. Furthermore, counselors must develop their written communication skills: they must be able to provide appropriate, clear, concise, and legible documentation that incorporates information from diverse relevant sources.

As part of their communications skills, counselors must be able to prepare and present oral and written assessment findings to the client and other professionals, even while applying confidentiality regulations. As part of assessments, counselors need to explain recommendations to the client and any other participants in the process, including service providers. Above all, counselors need to transmit information clearly.

Attitudes

Counselors need to maintain a respectful attitude towards the assessment as an integral part of mapping out the appropriate treatment for the client. At the same time, counselors must appreciate the limits of assessment instruments and interpretation; assessing a client is a holistic process.

Counselors must maintain professionalism at all times. This includes accepting their own limitations as appropriate.

Counselors must always appreciate the value of accurate documentation.

Person-Centered Treatment Planning and Co-Occurring Mental Disorders

A patient's person-centered change plan must take into consideration special circumstances such as cultural, sexual, and spiritual beliefs. Part of this process is to detect issues and developmental delays that occur due to a lack of life skill techniques.

For effective person-centered treatment, the counselor should involve family if possible, as well as identify an alternate plan. Experts who study the process of recovery from addiction have determined that family involvement is an important part of the recovery process, so it should be implemented whenever possible. Person-centered therapy has shown to be most effective when the counselor involves the family in both the assessment and planning process of the treatment and recovery.

Another aspect of person-centered treatment involves providing educational processes that revolve around continued recovery. To do this, the counselor can use groups for peer support. Addicts often lack proper support, so providing users with peers whom they can rely on will help them through the process of recovery by relating to others.

For person-centered therapy, the counselor should use caution when discussing any type of medication with the patient who is in recovery. The patient must also be educated on use and harm-reduction techniques that they can use to help reduce harm to themselves and reduce their amount of use.

An important aspect of person-centered treatment involves arranging care with a case manager. During treatment, the case manager helps the patient to develop the skills needed to find employment and survive independently without drugs once the treatment program is over. The case manager should ensure that the plan created between the counselor and the patient is sensitive to the patient's individual needs.

Co-Occurring Mental Disorders

A "dual diagnosis" patient, one who suffers from both substance abuse and a mental disorder, requires a unique treatment plan. By implementing the proper treatment plan for co-occurring mental disorders, the process of recovery will be much easier for the individual and he or she will have a much greater chance of success.

Mental illness could cause the patient to resist treatment approaches. Depending on the type of mental disorder present, the patient may think of the treatment center as a negative place, leading to withdrawal and relapse.

Issues Regarding Dual Approach

Part of the counselor's job when dealing with co-occurring mental disorders is recognizing that both issues need to be addressed during the treatment process. By addressing only substance use, true mental health issues can be overlooked and can trigger the substance use to come back. By addressing both issues at once, the probability of recovery from drugs and alcohol abuse increases greatly.

To assist a patient with co-occurring mental disorders, the counselor must work to help the patient to find a group with these common issues. For example, those suffering from depression may be able to better relate with the group that offers support for patients with both depression and substance abuse issues.

The counselor should have a psychiatric medication administered to the patient when applicable, after a psychiatric evaluation by a medical professional. The medication may help the cravings of the substance addiction, as it works to address both issues.

Configuration Styles

- Gentle approach - A less forceful approach to recovery may offer better results for some patients.

- Multiple intervention approach - Use of multiple intervention techniques will help when the patient is reluctant to accept their mental disorder.

- Unique approach - When substance abuse and a mental disorder are present, a unique treatment plan must be used for the patient. The method used is unique when compared to the process of treatment for someone with only an addiction problem.

Case Management Principles and Techniques

Case managers and counselors are two separate types of support for the patient recovering from addiction. By incorporating case management and counselor techniques, a single entry of progression regarding the patient is incorporated. Lack of proper incorporation of case management and counseling techniques can create barriers between systems that could affect the recovery process for the patient, a lack of agreement on a plan, and a lack of infinitives for progression.

Treatment Models

There are different models involved in the treatment process, which involve using both case management and counselor techniques in order to provide proper patient care. These models provide effective treatment, and the different approaches used help the patient in all areas of life.

Assertive Community Therapy Model

Assertive community therapy provides a wide range of therapy services and helps to implement the services into the patient's everyday life. This therapy includes job assistance, skills building, and other valuable resources. The assertive community therapy model:

- Has seven areas of emphasis.

- Creates a natural setting for client care. For example, the care may be provided in home for the patient or in a familiar environment.

- Focuses on activities of daily living.

- Creates asserted advocacy.

- Involves continuous and frequent client contact between the case managers and the counselor.

- Involves shared cases that use team products.

- Creates long-term communication between the case manager and the counselor during the patient's treatment process.

- Focuses on mental health as well as addresses substance abuse treatment options.

Broker Generalist Model

The most basic type of case management, the broker generalist model allows the case manager to detect problems and provide necessary services. It is considered the most effective model when treatment providers and social service workers require additional information regarding the patient.

Process Treatment Model

In the process treatment model, the patient agrees to treatment when he or she "hits bottom," rather than being forced into treatment. This model supports the patient's transition to treatment. It also focuses on patient strengths and expands upon them by encouraging and developing a helping network, creating a strong case management and client relationship, and providing active and aggressive care for the patient at all times.

Strategy-Based Model

The strategy-based model supports patients with mental illnesses transfer from inpatient or outpatient facilities. The counselor offers support by providing resources to the client in terms of housing, employment, and social support resources. This model is designed to help clients use their own strengths as a tool to acquire the resources they need in order to have a successful recovery.

Clinical Rehabilitation Therapy Model

Clinical rehabilitation therapy connects clinical treatment with case management. The case manager addresses issues regarding client services, which can include life skills, psychotherapy, and family therapy. Both types of treatment can be used on their own and combined together to gain optimal results and determine the progression of the patient. The clinical rehabilitation therapy model is a combined approach, and thought to be an effective strategy for patients with co-occurring mental disorders.

Case Management Model

Applied to help patients see and address issues that they may have, the case management model helps develop a motor for change in the patient's new skills, which is used to implement the necessary change. Once a plan for change is designed by the case manager, the patient is encouraged to apply these techniques to daily life. Engagement encourages the patient to reach out for help when necessary.

Case Management Techniques

Case management techniques, which should be applied during pre-treatment, include:

- Providing resources to the patient that not only help with the transition but also help the person to live a better life. For example, developing and maintaining social relationships.

- Properly addressing issues during treatment process.

- Offering safe housing and addressing substance abuse issues during the pretreatment phase.

- Addressing issues such as anger, lack of understanding, and mental health service denial. This will ensure that recovery is more successful when the patient enters the treatment phase.

- Detecting and addressing problems not previously addressed. For example, a minimalist may not perceive any negative consequences from his or her substance abuse, or behave as such, which will make treatment ineffective.

- Detecting issues such as missed appointments, continued substance use, multiple excuses, no commitment to recovery, and apathy.

Primary Treatment

Primary treatment techniques aim to help the patient make a delicate transition in all areas of the treatment process together. This is done prior to leaving the inpatient program. Primary treatment addresses the aftercare needs of the patient during the primary phase of therapy. For example, housing needs, follow-up treatment program issues, support systems, financial needs, and health issues all are things that will need to be addressed for aftercare.

With primary treatment, the counselor must address the dental and medical needs of the patient. Often, dental and medical care is offered for the first time in years during primary treatment, so proper monitoring of the medication should be done at all times. Counselors and case managers must work as advocates during health treatment for the patient.

The Primary Treatment Assessment Process

Focusing on addiction treatment and identifying various patient needs for common services are done during the assessment process. This involves:

- Detecting special skills or defects within the patient.

- Providing basic supplemental needs to the patient.

- Identifying the level of regular ability to function with the patient.

- Detecting various patient risk strategies.

Primary Treatment Results

Treatment results are generated by the patient with the help of the counselor and/or case manager. Treatment can be effective when:

- An effective service plan is created.

- Treatment occurs in a forward motion during the recovery phases.

- Support is provided when transitioning from the inpatient and outpatient program.

- Issues are addressed while using residential treatment program.

- Both the patient and the counselor start the treatment program through the use of primary treatment.

Primary Treatment Goals

Goals for primary treatment are developed collaboratively by the patient and case manager. In order to make both long- and short-term goals, the counselor must:

- Offer continued motivation to the patient in order to engage in positive progression in the treatment process.

- Determine the proper timing of application of service to get appropriate treatment.

- Offer support to the patient during the transitional phase.

- Use intervention to avoid crises and respond when appropriate.

- Provide the patient with the skills needed for independence.

- Create an external support structure to facilitate independence, and use community integration.

Primary Treatment Techniques

The techniques used by the counselor reduce both external and internal patient barriers. The plan created must be used directly after the assessment process. When used with the patient, this plan includes:

- Planning for proper treatment.

- Setting goals.

- Implementing the goals. This is most effective when broken up into smaller goals by creating objectives, outlining steps, and determining the objects of goals.

Failure to meet a goal allows the patients the chance to assess the situation and to reevaluate their approach to meeting the goal; they can then determine how to change that approach in order to achieve the goal.

Treatment Planning

During treatment, the counselor and client work together to decide upon goals, or treatment outcomes, and how to reach them. A treatment plan should encompass and interpret assessment data; further, it must approach and confront the specific substance abuse disorder or disorders affecting the client. Treatment also addresses possible factors and impediments to progress in treatment like family and other significant relationships; and health, legal, education, employment, and spiritual problems and needs.

Knowledge

In treatment planning, counselors should be cognizant of the entire treatment planning process, including stages of change and readiness for treatment, client's level of motivation and interest in making specific changes, and processes and factors of motivation. Counselors must be familiar with the hierarchy of needs; the relationships among client needs and problems; the diverse treatment needs and challenges of varying populations; and relationships among problems, desired outcomes, and treatment strategies. Furthermore, knowledge of the stages of change models and methodology of evaluating treatment and stages of recovery is essential.

As during the assessment process, counselors must account for the role and importance of client resources and barriers to treatment. Counselors need a knowledge of the impact that the client and family systems have on treatment decisions and outcomes, including any roles that significant others may play in treatment and intervention strategies. As such, it is essential that the counselor recognize the importance of client's racial or ethnic culture, age, developmental level, gender, and life circumstances, accounting for these factors in coordinating resources to client needs.

Counselors must be knowledgeable of other sources of assessment information. Available treatment modalities, client placement criteria, and cost issues all affect the treatment planning process. A strong knowledge of the effectiveness of the various treatment models based on current research will help the counselor tailor treatment to the needs of the client; awareness of the implications of various treatment alternatives, including no treatment, is also part of the individualized approach. Counselors should be knowledgeable about treatment modalities, treatment sequencing, the continuum of care, and community resources.

As part of the continuum of care, counselors need a background in the contributions of other professions and mutual-help or self-help support groups. They require a knowledge of current placement criteria. Counselors must know and adhere to federal, state, and agency confidentiality regulations, requirements, and policies at all times. They must be aware of resources for legal consultation.

Skills

In the treatment setting, all counselors need effective communication styles. Counselors should be prepared to make the most of their skills in negotiating, problem solving, and engaging and contracting with others (relationship building). It is imperative to establish trusting relationships in order to work collaboratively. In treatment, proper timing, sequencing, and prioritizing is key; counselors require strong organizational skills.

Counselors should know how to plan treatment in both the short- and long-term, including how to write measurable outcome statements and develop timelines for reviewing and revising treatment plans. To do this, counselors must translate assessment information into (measurable) treatment goals and outcomes, summarizing and synthesizing assessment results, then synthesizing the available data to establish treatment priorities. Adhering to confidentiality regulations and standards of practice, counselors communicate assessment findings to interested parties.

Counselors must present all information in a non-judgmental manner and focus on promoting the client's readiness to accept treatment. It is paramount to ensure that the client understands assessment findings and the reasoning behind treatment recommendations and priorities; ensure that the client for understands and correct any misunderstandings. Counselors must explain the treatment process and develop strategies to overcome communications barriers.

Developing individual treatment plans with the client means tailoring them to the client, balancing his or her own strengths and weaknesses. As circumstances change, counselors need to modify the treatment plan as necessary (depending on client progress). Counselors will help choose those treatment settings most appropriate for specific client needs and preferences, keeping in mind the client's preferences and discussions with the client about common treatment goals.

As always, communication is key in treatment. Counselors must acclimate to clients of different age, racial and ethnic background, sexual orientation, gender identity, developmental level, and other categories, taking into account their unique perspectives when communicating with them.

Counselors will work with the client to develop realistic time frames for completing goals; as such, counselors must engage, contract, and negotiate with the client in this collaborative process. It follows that counselors must identify alternate approaches tailored to client needs as needed. Part of treatment is implementing strategies in terms understandable to the client: to a great extent, the treatment process entails collaborating and contracting with the client to create an action plan in positive, proactive terms. Furthermore, counselors establish criteria to evaluate progress. Relationship building is essential; counselors build partnerships with the client and his or her significant others. In addition, counselors must communicate the roles of various interested parties and support systems and elicit feedback on the treatment process. Counselors respond to questions and clarify as needed.

Counselors must be able to explain client rights and responsibilities and applicable regulations regarding confidentiality. Counselors must be able to refer to the appropriate legal authority when needed.

Attitudes

As in all aspects of counseling, recognition of one's own treatment biases is important: treatment must be tailored to the needs of the client, so counselors must be willing to consider multiple approaches to recovery and change and coordinate them in treatment. Counselors should value professional collaboration as permitted by confidentiality regulations. They should remain willing to accept professional feedback and to learn from clinical supervision, modifying practice accordingly.

In general, counselors should always have respect for the client, other significant people and their roles in the client's treatment, and the client's own values and goals. Counselors must remain sensitive to point of view of client (including gender, cultural, and other issues), his or her goals, and pace of change in treatment, promoting the value of achieving even small goals. Counselors should understand the value of monitoring treatment outcomes. Counselors should value and promote the strengths of clients and significant others and be aware of their limitations.

Counselors must recognize the client's right and need to understand assessment results and examine treatment implications in collaboration with the client and significant others, respecting their input. Counselors must demonstrate willingness to negotiate with the client at all times, as well as a willingness to communicate interactively with the client and significant others.

At all times, counselors must demonstrate their commitment to professionalism, including patience and perseverance (being thorough and following through on commitments).

Stress Management

Counselors are at high risk for burnout in any field, and those caring for recovering addicts are no exception. People with substance abuse issues and those with mental health disorders come from all backgrounds. They may be suffering from the aftereffects of their addiction and accompanying lifestyle and continue to behave in a difficult manner. They and their families may be confused, frightened, and difficult as a result. Some clients will have undergone harrowing experiences that can be uncomfortable and saddening to discuss. In order to maintain empathy, taking self-care actions is critical for a counselor's success in this field. These include:

- Recognizing negative thought patterns. This is important because negative thoughts can slow down or alter the process of treatment for the patient.

- Recognizing these emotions allows the counselor to identify personal reactions and change thoughts by practicing coping techniques for stress and negative thinking.

- The counselor must continue examination of these negative thought patterns each time they occur in a negative manner in order to achieve the highest level of results.

Self-Care and Stress Reduction

- Consider a view of various certification components and sign a timeframe to achieve different components.

- Make your goals realistic.

- Examine various stages of stress and determine the cause of the stress.

- Memorize a positive statement and make progress.

- Don't aim for perfection. Regard your effort more than the outcome.

- Use the "one step at a time" strategy.

- Care for your mind by relaxing during stressful times.

- Care for your body by spending time with a supportive circle and expressing your emotions.

- Care for your spirit by learning to forgive yourself during times of failure and implementing positive thinking during this time.

- Utilize resources available within the community to help prevent negative consequences due to overexertion. For example, negative emotions and burnout are related to overexertion and can be worked upon with in the professional community with those who offer support.

Community-Based Stress Prevention

To help a client deal with stress, the counselor can use community-based stress prevention. These prevention tactics include:

- Developing a strong support system within the community, particularly with people with similar beliefs as yours. Within the group, your behaviors tend to become similar to the behaviors of others.

- Create a group outside of the mental health system for support

Benefits of Community-Based Support

Community-based principles have shown to be effective, including benefits provided by:

- Compassion
- Commitment
- Involvement
- Leadership
- Communication affect
- Problem-solving

Referral

During the clinical evaluation and/or treatment planning, the counselor and client identify the client's needs. As a result, the counselor may provide a referral, which is a way to guide the client to other available resources and support systems to meet those needs. Referrals address client needs and service gaps by connecting agencies, governmental bodies, civic groups, and other treatment professionals, expanding community resources.

The counselor must have an understanding of the mission, function, resources, and quality of services offered by many community based organizations. These include: civic groups, community groups, and neighborhood organizations; religious organizations; governmental entities; health and allied health care systems (managed care); criminal justice systems; housing administrations; employment and vocational rehabilitation services; child care facilities; crisis intervention programs; abused persons programs; mutual and self-help groups; cultural enhancement organizations; advocacy groups; and other agencies.

Knowledge

The counselor must be familiar with community demographics—specifically, the political and cultural systems of the community, and the needs of those served. Furthermore, the counselor requires an in-depth knowledge of the specific criteria for receiving community services; it follows that he or she must also know how to access service providers and agencies, including financial details. Counselors should be able to find the most current information regarding referral criteria, services offered, resources, accreditation status, and client satisfaction of service providers in the community. Above all, they should be able to tailor recommendations to the needs of the individual client.

Ensuring an individualized approach to referrals as part of treatment means ensuring client follow-up: counselors should educate clients on the referral process, motivate them to initiate the referral process and to follow through with recommendations and commitments. The counselor should identify the factors in treatment that determine the best time to engage the client in the referral process; moreover, the counselor must ensure that the client has the necessary access and logistics to follow through on referrals him- or herself. Counselors should keep the client's cultural influences, appearance, presentation abilities, and defenses in mind: all these factors affect follow-through on referrals. Counselors must have a strong knowledge of those methods used to assess client progress toward desired treatment outcomes, knowing how treatment planning and referrals connect to the overall goals in recovery. Counselors should also be aware of the rights and responsibilities of the client. Finally, counselors must be able to evaluate referral outcomes, knowledgeable of the sources and techniques for doing so.

Counselors should be able to identify gaps in service and be able to advocate for new resources as appropriate. They should know state and federal legislative mandates and regulations and be able to apply appropriate confidentiality regulations and protocols. Counselors must be familiar with referral terminology and structure and comfortable with referral protocols and necessary documentation. Counselors need a strong knowledge of the standards of ethics that apply to information exchange in the referral process. They must also know how to access key resource persons in community service provider network.

Finally, counselors must know and adhere to local, state, and federal confidentiality regulations, client consent procedures, and other standards guiding information exchange.

Skills

In community-based prevention, counselors must advocate for clients, requiring networking and communications skills, including strong oral and written communications abilities. Effective communication in the referral process more broadly includes education of clients, negotiating (both with clients and partners), and personalizing the risks and benefits of referrals. Counselors must use the correct terminology in obtaining and providing client information to partners in the referrals process. At the same time, counselors must utilize terminology and function in language that the client will understand in order to personalize treatment, educate the client, and appropriately obtain the necessary information (and documentation) in accordance with confidentiality regulations.

Counselors need to cooperate with others as part of a team. This means counselors must maintain and nourish key relationships in the treatment community, in part by providing feedback to partners in regards to service delivery. Counselors must be able to utilize shared resources connecting treatment partners such as directories and digital databases. Counselors must be capable of collecting data on the referrals process and continuously assess and reassess referrals and the process to determine whether they are appropriate for the specific client and his or her treatment objectives.

As regards the referral process, counselors must be able to determine whether referral is appropriate by interpreting assessment, treatment planning, evaluation, and client feedback data. Furthermore, counselors must objectively assess the client's readiness and willingness to engage not only in treatment but also in the referral process and educate him or her in that process. Readiness and education includes motivating clients to actively participate in the referral process by being responsible for following through on the referral and following up. Moreover, counselors measure follow-up with the client with specific processes and instruments, reporting information accurately. Counselors must be able to understand how referrals relate and contribute to progress in the treatment plan overall.

Attitudes

As in all treatment counseling, counselors must retain attitudes of respect, open-mindedness, and professionalism. Counselors should appreciate cooperation in general. Counselors must value the interdisciplinary nature of service delivery, inter-agency collaboration, referral, and the evaluation process. Furthermore, counselors should understand and value the need to share information with other professional partners (in line with confidentiality regulations). In general, counselors must appreciate professional standards and adhere to confidentiality regulations at all times. Overall, counselors should have patience, perseverance, and a commitment to professionalism at all times.

Respect extends to client needs in interaction with outside agencies. Counselors must retain the client's perspective, taking into account client needs and agency services and maintaining a willingness to advocate for the client as necessary. Counselors should consistently value holistic, interdisciplinary, inter-agency approaches to assisting clients meet positive treatment outcomes, staying aware of their own potential biases toward or against referral resources.

Counselors should be willing to collaborate in decision-making with the client and respect the client's capabilities in taking ownership of the referral (initiating and following up). Maintaining an attitude of collaboration and respect promotes the client's needs and positive self-determination. At the same time, counselors should recognize their responsibility to engage in client advocacy when it may be necessary.

Service Coordination

In service coordination, the client and the service agencies—treatment services, local agencies, and other resources—come together to target the clinical, evaluative, administrative, and other needs identified in the treatment plan. Service coordination allows clients to achieve specific treatment objectives. It includes case management; client advocacy; collaborating not only with the client, but also his or her significant others; coordinating treatment and referral services; connecting community resources and managed care systems; and continuing assessment of treatment progress and needs of the client. Collaboration with a referral source is key to implement treatment plans.

Knowledge

For optimum service coordination, counselors must know the missions, functions, and resources in the available local service network and understand the managed care and other systems affecting the client. They must be familiar with the various philosophies, policies, procedures, and admissions protocols of every agency they work with. They must understand the terminology and methodology used by service providers and in the coordination environment. Furthermore, they need to be able to understand client- and treatment-related information as it pertains to service coordination specifically. As such, they must be strongly familiar with the methodology of documentation and reporting used by various partner agencies and the protocols of managed care organizations.

As always, counselors must understand the principles to tailor treatment to the client's specific needs. In service coordination, counselors must understand what makes a client eligible for referral to service providers—eligibility and admission criteria as well as protocols—and know how to identify, find, and transmit the necessary information for referral. They must know and understand the federal, state, and local regulations for admissions. They require a strong knowledge of case presentation and protocols.

Furthermore, counselors should be familiar with ways to evaluate and track the client's status and changes throughout the treatment process. Thus they must be familiar with the specific services and programs offered by service providers and managed care systems, including treatment schedules and timeframes, discharge criteria, and rules and regulations. Counselors also require a knowledge of the cost of treatment programs as part of service coordination, including available mechanisms for funding, protocols for reimbursement and rates, how finances impact treatment, and the required documentation.

General knowledge that applies to substance abuse counselors also applies in service coordination, including knowledge of federal and state confidentiality regulations, when it is appropriate to apply them, and documentation requirements. Counselors should fully understand the roles (and limits) of the client's family and significant others in treatment. Counselors require a broad knowledge of client rights and responsibilities.

From a more theoretical standpoint, counselors working in service coordination should have a background in the theoretical concepts and philosophy behind screening and assessment, especially the tools used in those processes. They should also understand biopsychosocial assessment methods. Counselors should be able to articulate treatment goals (both long and short term). Counselors should know and practice effective communication styles.

Skills

Service coordination requires negotiation. Counselors must be able to interact and negotiate with varying treatment systems. Networking is also key: counselors need to build relationships with community partners, generating trust and establishing a rapport. Collaborative skills are important for participation in interdisciplinary team building. In general, counselors require skills in negotiation, mediation, conflict resolution, problem solving, and advocacy. Counselors must be skilled in advocating for client services.

Service coordination requires technological and communicative skill. Counselors must be able to collect information from varying sources on client treatment and interpret it accurately, using the proper technology. Furthermore, they must be comfortable with the technology used to transmit client data for referrals and that used for documentation. Counselors must be able to communicate clearly, accurately and concisely in both oral and written communication. Counselors should be able to deliver case presentations. Counselors should be able to utilize and be familiar with inter-agency terminology, but they must also be able to use language that the client will understand. Counselors should be able to access financial resources as necessary.

The counselor must be skilled at eliciting information from diverse sources including the client, and he or she must prioritize, understand, and appropriately use that information in service coordination. Counselors must determine the level of care needed and its intensity through appropriate assessments and work with the client to plan treatment. Family and other significant members of the client's social system should be involved; furthermore, counselors must be able to demonstrate respect for cultural differences. At the same time, counselors must be able to respectfully set boundaries with the client and significant others. Counselors must be able to recognize and convey client change.

103

Attitudes

Counselors should value diversity in systems and approaches to treatment and remain open minded to alternative approaches. Counselors should value information of all types and from all sources as well as its possible implications for treatment. Furthermore, counselors must understand and accept the need to work within or partner with bureaucratic systems. Overall, counselors working in service coordination must demonstrate patience, perseverance, and a willingness to collaborate and cooperate.

Counselors must appreciate clients' need for ongoing encouragement and consistent support; to this end, counselors should maintain an optimistic attitude. Counselors should demonstrate value for client self-reporting and self-assessment, appreciating self-determination as an objective. However, counselors should also be aware of any personal biases that could impact their work and be willing to accept treatment limitations that may affect some clients. Counselors should respect the need to assess and modify the treatment plan on an ongoing basis. Finally, as in other elements of substance abuse counseling, counselors should demonstrate respect for the contribution of the client's family and significant others to the process.

Consulting

Consulting may play a role in the course of treatment. Consulting ensures a high quality of care by reviewing the treatment plan, the client's progress, and taking stock of any problems inhibiting progress, all keeping the client's background in mind. Consulting also allows the counselors to gather feedback and adjust the treatment plan as appropriate.

Knowledge

Consulting requires a strong knowledge of assessment methods. Consultants know the following methodologies: assessing the client's biopsychosocial status (both past and present); those social systems that may affect his or her progress; and those for ongoing assessment of the treatment plan and modification if necessary.

In consulting, counselors must be knowledgeable about related disciplines, including any unique language and terminology used and various functions. They should understand the primary functions of other team members within their own disciplines, including their responsibilities and specialties. In general, consulting demands a deep knowledge of teamwork and appropriate behaviors within a professional group setting.

Finally, understanding and following confidentiality procedures in consulting is imperative. Counselors and consultants must know and understand all local, state, and federal confidentiality laws and regulations and know how to apply them in sharing information and documentation regarding clients. They must also be aware of client rights and responsibilities. Furthermore, they should know the ethical and professional standards applicable to confidentiality.

Skills

In consulting, communication and relationship-building skills are key. Like other elements of counseling, consulting requires written and verbal communication skills: professionals must be able to speak and write clearly, accurately and concisely. They must adhere to confidentiality regulations in communicating with service providers, clients, and clients' family and significant others; counselors must also be able to explain confidentiality regulations to other parties as needed. Counselors must build and nourish relationships with both clients and community partners, remaining objective and respectful. They should ask for feedback regarding the treatment plan and client satisfaction and remain open to outside perspectives.

Counselors working with clients in consulting modify treatment plans as needed in coordination with other service providers and the client to help clients more effectively reach treatment goals. Consulting requires the ability to obtain, interpret, and synthesize information from various sources in order to evaluate and modify treatment objectives. Counselors must be able to prioritize and document that client data relevant to the consulting process; to do so, they must have the ability to identify challenges to progress. Furthermore, counselors need to obtain informed consent from the client, ensuring that the client understands the process at hand.

Counselors working in consulting must be skilled in professional and interdisciplinary collaboration in order to coordinate client treatment with various representatives within the multidisciplinary framework. Counselors will utilize problem solving, decision making, mediation, and advocacy skills in a collaborative, interdisciplinary setting in consulting. They should actively participate in team building activities. Finally, in interacting with interagency partners, counselors must be able to transmit information about clients professionally, following applicable confidentiality regulations and professional standards.

Attitudes

Consultants should always maintain respect for the client, the client's right to privacy, and the privacy of the information shared by the client and his or her significant others. When interacting on behalf of the client with service providers, counselors should maintain a respectful and non-judgmental attitude regarding the client at all times, advocating for his or her interests. As a client advocate, the counselor's attitude should be one of professional concern. As in other elements of counseling, in consulting counselors should appreciate incremental changes and recognize relapse as an opportunity for change rather than a failure.

In the collaborative professional setting, counselors must always demonstrate respect for the interdisciplinary nature of consulting work, showing interest in professional collaboration with partners. Counselors should be at ease sharing information and asking questions. They should always remain appreciative of the contributions of other team members and respect their professional roles and backgrounds.

In consulting as in all other specialties counselors must always respect confidentiality regulations and apply them as necessary; they should always maintain high professional standards.

Continued Assessment and Planning

Continued assessment and planning involves maintaining ongoing contact with client and involving significant others to ensure adherence to the treatment plan.

Knowledge

For continued assessment and planning, counselors need expertise in outreach, follow-up, and aftercare techniques. Counselors will engage the client in the ongoing treatment process and need to know the techniques to facilitate this process, including methods for determining the client's goals, treatment plan, and motivational level. To do so, counselors must also know how to identify and evaluate client motivation and client progress toward treatment goals and objectives. Overall, they must have a strong understanding of the continuum of care.

As in other aspects of treatment, counselors require a knowledge of relapse prevention strategies. They must recognize the signs and symptoms of relapse and master methods for re-involving the client in the treatment planning process if necessary.

As in other elements of counseling, counselors require expertise in assessment mechanisms to measure client's progress toward treatment objectives and should be knowledgeable about the stages of the treatment and recovery process. Counselors need a strong knowledge of the modalities of measuring outcomes. They should be mindful of individual differences in the recovery process and able to identify those factors that may affect the client's success in treatment.

Of course, the counselor needs expertise in treatment planning. Given the ongoing nature of continued assessment and planning, counselors should be comfortable with the treatment planning process in accordance with the continuum of care. They require knowledge of the criteria for admissions and placement as appropriate, as well as varying treatment modalities. Counselors should be familiar with methods for evaluating treatment progress and client status, including documentation of process, progress, and outcome. They should also understand the role of service providers in the treatment process.

Counselors should know the methods for measuring outcomes and how to ascertain the validity of those measurements. They should have a strong knowledge of discharge indicators and the discharge planning process. As part of discharge, counselors should be aware of the client's available social and family systems for continuing care, as well as the resources available in his or her community resources.

In general, counselors should master interviewing techniques. Furthermore, they need a broad knowledge of documentation requirements including those related to addiction counseling, agencies and service providers, funding sources, and others.

A knowledge of the theoretical philosophies and perspectives on social, cultural, and family systems is helpful in continued assessment and planning; counselors should also review current theoretical perspectives on stages of change.

Skills

Counselors continue to tailor treatment to clients' needs even beyond the immediate treatment setting. To do so, they must use methods for measuring progress and treatment objectives. Counselors will work with referral sources, collecting relevant information on clients. They advocate for clients, assisting them in obtaining placement and identifying admissions and discharge criteria as appropriate. Counselors must help the client create a relapse prevention plan and stay motivated in recovery. Counselors are responsible for ensuring follow-up and aftercare protocols are implemented.

Again, communication is key, and recovery is a process. When working in continued assessment and planning, the counselor will be engaging the client and his or her social support system in the ongoing process of treatment, including continuing care. Thus the counselor needs to build a lasting relationship and sustained contact with these figures. Counselors should observe and account for the level of comprehension the client and social system have for the treatment process; furthermore, they should take into account cultural barriers and other differences in perspective. Counselors should always solicit clients' feedback and thoughts on their own progress. Finally, it is important to recognize and address ambivalence and resistance to the ongoing process as part of monitoring the client's commitment to the treatment plan.

As part of these relationships, counselors may be called upon to assist in resolving conflicts or solving problems, acting as mediators. Counselors require negotiating skills. Counselors must reinforce and encourage positive change; the counselor assesses, recognizes, and documents milestones and progress.

Specific skills in maintaining these ongoing relationships include interviewing clients, groups, and families; documenting steps the client takes indicating commitment to the treatment plan and treatment progress; and being able to identify and document change. To accomplish this, counselors require accurate, clear, and concise verbal and written communication skills (as in other aspects of counseling). Furthermore, they must know how to use the appropriate reporting technology, adhering to timelines and confidentiality regulations. They should be able to identify, obtain and prioritize the relevant information from diverse sources pertaining to the client's ongoing treatment.

Attitudes

In continued assessment and planning, counselors must hold similar attitudes as in other elements of counseling. Counselors should maintain general attitudes of therapeutic optimism, remaining flexible and patient. As in other aspects of counseling, they must appreciate the importance of accurate documentation as an integral part of the treatment process, recognizing the value of monitoring progress and measuring outcomes. Counselors must be able and willing to use appropriate technology and stay current regarding relevant technological innovations.

Counselors should respect and appreciate individual differences, especially in the recovery process; furthermore, they should appreciate the role significant others play in the recovery process. As such, counselors should recognize the cultural issues that may impact ongoing treatment progress. Above all, counselors need to respect the client's right to self-determination. It is the counselor's job to appreciate and present relapse as motivation for reinvigorated recovery.

As part of the multidisciplinary context of community-based prevention, counselors should value treatment planning in the interdisciplinary context. They must have confidence in the client's ability to progress within a continuum of care and appreciate the fair and objective use of client placement, continued stay, and discharge criteria.

Client, Family, and Community Education

In client, family, and community education, counselors educate these parties about the risks, prevention, and treatment of substance abuse. Education includes culturally sensitive formal and informal programs to raise awareness and promote prevention and recovery in families and the community.

Knowledge

It should be no surprise that counselors working in client, family, and community education should know how to develop and present educational programs; to do so, counselors need expertise in pedagogical methodology and different styles of learning. They need an in-depth background in the current theory and research on social approaches to substance abuse prevention. Furthermore, they should have a knowledge of current public policy in their community on substance abuse treatment and prevention.

Counselors working in education must recognize the warning signs of a substance abuse disorder and understand the continuum of use and abuse. They need a strong understanding of the various models used for the prevention of substance abuse disorders, as well as those for substance abuse treatment and recovery. Furthermore, counselors must be deeply familiar with the research and theory supporting those models. Finally, counselors require a knowledge of the relevant diagnostic standards (including DSM categories) regarding substance abuse.

As in other aspects of community-based prevention, counselors need a knowledge of the continuum of care in general and of specific treatment resources available locally. These may include local health, allied health, community health, and behavioral health resources, among others. In addition, counselors should have an understanding of the influences on social and political responses to substance abuse disorders.

Other social issues to which counselors must be sensitive when working in the community include cultural diversity within communities, taking into account cultural divisions within and among ethnically and racially diverse communities. These differences affect consumption of psychoactive substances and the perception of substance use disorders. Furthermore, counselors must be aware of the local social issues that could be influencing the development of substance abuse disorders in the community, both in general (such as age and gender differences in substance abuse) as well as across cultural lines. Counselors must develop an understanding of how the local environment influences the risk of substance abuse disorders within a community and a community's resilience to their development. Counselors should have some background in resources for substance abuse prevention, treatment and recovery appropriate for local culture, taking into account age, gender, and other factors relevant in the community.

Counselors must also understand the family dynamics of substance abuse, including the effect of substance abuse on family members and significant figures in an addict's life. Moreover, counselors require a deep understanding of the potential for the addict's family to influence the development of his or her substance use disorder (in either a positive or negative way). As in other aspects of substance abuse counseling, counselors require a knowledge of how an addict's social system influences his or her recovery and what role family members and significant others can play in treatment.

In general, counselors need a general knowledge of the health risks associated with substance use. They must be able to identify the high-risk behaviors related to substance use. They must understand how infectious diseases are transmitted and prevented, including associated factors.

One of the best ways to prevent and to treat substance abuse disorders is a strong grasp of life skills like stress management, communication, and boundary-setting. Counselors must understand these skills and know how to teach them in both the individual and group setting. Counselors should have a knowledge of the resources locally available to aid in teaching life skills.

Skills

Counselors working in education must be able to organize and deliver public presentations that reflect basic information on prevention, treatment, and recovery. Communicating effectively with diverse populations in both formal and informal settings is a must; therefore, counselors must be comfortable with public speaking and able to facilitate small and large group discussions. Counselors must be able to effectively implement training sessions. They must create educational materials for public distribution; in addition, they should be able to identify and access other instructional resources to enrich the training.

As counselors are educating clients, families, and the community, they must be able to tailor their presentations to focus on the impact of substance use disorders on the family, couple, or significant others. This means providing educational programs that reflect understanding of culture, ethnicity, age, and gender. It is important to teach the symptoms of various substance use disorders and to facilitate discussions about these warning signs. Counselors should explain the broader philosophy and principles supporting addiction prevention, treatment, and recovery. Counselors should explain what the continuum of care is and available resources to family and other members of the addict's social system. Furthermore, counselors should describe individual, community, and group risk and resiliency factors, discussing how the community can capitalize on these assets.

Motivating both family members and clients to seek care. Describing different treatment modalities and the continuum of care. Identifying and making referrals to local health, allied health, and behavioral health resources. Teaching clients and community members about disease transmission and prevention.

Attitudes

As educators, counselors must understand and value the difference between simply providing information and educating. They must always present issues in a non-judgmental fashion, remaining aware of their own biases. As in other aspects of the field, counselors must remain patient and professional.

Given the complex historical, social, cultural, and other influences on perceptions of psychoactive substance use, counselors must exhibit sensitivity to these specific factors in the local environment where they are serving. Indeed, counselors must remain aware of group, community, and individual differences in general that contribute to increased risk for substance use disorders. Furthermore, they must remain sensitive to the effects of age, gender, ethnicity, culture, and other factors in substance abuse prevention, treatment, and recovery in the local context. Counselors must bear in mind the difficulty for families and significant others to seek help. Counselors must appreciate the value of life skills training to strengthening recovery.

Addiction prevention and treatment are a cornerstone of community education; counselors need to appreciate the value of research in these fields. They must also recognize the importance of promoting prevention and treatment using multiple strategies.

Assessment & Psycho-Social-Spiritual Evaluation

- The counselor must develop the skills necessary to exhibit sensitivity to the patient during the initial assessment as well as during treatment in the aftercare process.

- The counselor must work closely with other professionals for optimal care of the recovering addict. This works by joining different techniques, in order to provide the best results.

- The counselor must provide treatment based on the unique needs of the patient, as this is the most vital part of the treatment process.

- All effective treatment programs must incorporate all therapies for the patient in order for the best results to occur.

- Appropriate changes must be made by different professionals working within the treatment program, and problems regarding mental health should be addressed.

- Through the treatment process, the counselor can properly address the different issues, and progressions can be noted.

Prevention and Stress Management

The prevention and stress management process involves regularly addressing feelings related to different areas of treatment, types of treatment, and negative emotions. Support groups are used to determine the appropriate way of preventing stress by working with others on a professional basis. These often involve long-term skill development. The patient must develop skills to reduce stress.

Clear Purpose and Goals

- Set out intervention objectives and strategies for the client.
- Identify needs of the community; clarify the objective and scope of the program.

- Periodically assess the client's mental health, treatment objectives, and strategies.

- Ensure crisis counseling is included in service delivery to client.

- Ensure adequate staff training on scope of practice and how to make referrals as necessary.

- Have staff provide feedback on data including program accomplishments and number of contacts.

- Ensure adequate staff training and orientation, including written descriptions of roles for each assignment setting.

Connecting Stress and Relapse

According to the National Institutes of Health, stress is a critical factor for using alcohol and drugs and a significant aspect of relapse. Treatment techniques to prevent relapse and manage stress include social support, developing coping skills, and adequate problem-solving abilities. SAMHSA reports that around 50 percent of persons recovering from drug or alcohol abuse will experience one relapse. Components that connect stress and relapse include:

- Lack of ability to handle social pressures

- Psychological and physical reminders of past use

- Frequent exposure to circumstances that lead to drug or alcohol use

- Insufficient skills for dealing with negative emotions or interpersonal conflict

Developing Coping Skills

One of the most important aspects of a client's recovery is the development of stress management techniques and adequate coping skills. Stress often arises from many situations that are detrimental to a person's health. For recovering addicts, stress is the impetus for relapse. A drug and alcohol treatment program will help the addict gain understanding of his or her individual triggers and learn how to handle those triggers in the future.

Stress Management Techniques

One way for a drug and alcohol counselor to assist a client with stress management is to help with the development of constructive hobbies and activities that do not involve substance use. Many clients struggle after they leave an addiction recovery center because they are thrust back into social circles and circumstances associated with substance abuse. The client will have an improved chance of recovery by cultivating activities that do not involve this harmful behavior and to avoid such temptations.

For a successful recovery, the client should identify high-risk situations that could lead to stress and relapse before he or she leaves the rehabilitation center. Exercise is one good way to relieve stress, as it helps to cope with challenging circumstances. Nutrition is also an important aspect to help the client deal with negative emotions while also enhancing his or her overall well-being.

Group, family, and individual counseling or therapy has proven advantageous for persons who have trouble handing stress and who are prone to relapse due to poor coping abilities. Clients should be encouraged to discuss these problems with other people who are struggling with recovery from substance use.

Relapse Prevention

Relapse is a progressive and negative pattern of behavior. Some common symptoms are listed below.

At first, the addict may exhibit signs of denial: he or she may begin to worry about his or her own health, safety, and well-being, yet deny those concerns.

This period of denial is usually followed by avoidant and defensive behaviors. Addicts may begin to tell themselves that they are "cured" from their disease, or become sure that they no longer have a substance abuse disorder. They may begin to display more concern for others than themselves. Generally behavioral changes at this point include defensiveness, increased impulsive and compulsive behaviors, and a tendency to isolate.

Without intervention, the crisis builds. Clients begin to exhibit tunnel vision or obsessiveness, becoming increasingly depressed. They are no longer engaged in constructive life planning; in fact, current plans begin to fail as addicts at this point are generally no longer following through on them.

At this point the addict enters a period of immobilization, characterized by wishful thinking as opposed to action. Rather than taking productive steps or engaging in planning, addicts in this phase feel hopeless, that problems cannot be solved; moreover, they may show an immature desire to be happy without any real goal or plan.

A period of confusion and overreaction follows this phase. Addicts may go through periods of confusion and anger, showing irritation with friends and loved ones and becoming easily angered, sometimes without visible triggers.

At this point, addicts usually enter a period of depression characterized by irregular eating and sleeping habits, lack of structure and motivation, and rejection of offers of help. Addicts feel helpless, powerless, and unsatisfied. They have almost always ceased attending Twelve Step meetings, or are only rarely appearing.

Usually at this point addicts recognize they have lost control of their recovery, feeling self-pity and a devastating loss of confidence. These feelings are accompanied by active dishonesty and strong thoughts of using drugs or alcohol. So they begin to reduce their options for resolving emotional and practical problems by discontinuing treatment. Here, addicts are often harboring unreasonable resentments and/or suffering from overwhelming negative feelings like anger, frustration and loneliness.

At this point, the acute episode of relapse will occur. The addict loses control of his or her behavior with at least one negative outcome, including the following:

- Degeneration in all life areas

- Use of alcohol or drugs

- Suicide attempt

- Emotional or physical collapse

- Psychiatric or stress-related illness

- Heightened risk of accidents

- Disruption or degeneration of social support systems

Professional Responsibility and Ethics

(45 Hours)

Overview

Ethics are complex when it comes to drug and alcohol addiction. Ethical practice for the alcoholism and substance abuse professional involves several steps that must be taken within the system to avoid problems or cause harm to the patient. The ethical principles are a set of principles that create moral decisions involving patient care and value to the patient during the care. Aspects of ethical practice include:

- *Moral decisions* - These are decisions made by a counselor in a manner that regards the patient's best interest. Decisions involve policy, the right attitude, and appropriate behaviors on a case-by-case basis.

- *Laws* - These are rules and regulations known as informal ethical decision-making policy regarding all substance abuse counselors.

- *Principles* - The principles involved with ethics are based on a vast understanding of the principles within the addictions field. According to the principle, just because something is legal doesn't mean it's ethical.

Counselors must understand the different issues that can occur within the counseling field and how various laws apply to the patient and the counselor. When working with patients in different states, counselors must consider each state and the specific area regulations regarding substance abuse and treatment in each state. This is done to determine the legal and ethical aspects around the situation.

Each state must provide a guideline containing specific information based on various state to state laws. Hard copies of ethical principles should be provided to all counselors and other professionals working within the field. The ethical guide contains informational education on the behavior that should take place within this position.

Several ethical issues are involved with behavioral stance, but there are three main areas of focuses. These include:

- Confidentiality issues

- Dual resistance

- Rebellion against legal and ethical issues.

Professionalism and Ethics

Professional and ethical responsibilities are the obligations of an addiction counselor to adhere to accepted ethical and behavioral standards of conduct and continuing professional development. Within this concept, the counselor must adhere to established professional codes of ethics that define the professional context within which the counselor works, in order to maintain professional standards and safeguard the client.

Knowledge

To maintain the highest professional and ethical standards, it is essential that counselors are aware of and adhere to confidentiality regulations. Furthermore, they must be aware of the legal ramifications of non-compliance with confidentiality regulations. They require a strong knowledge of client rights and responsibilities and the legal ramifications of violating client rights. Counselors should know how to voice professional concerns and understand grievance processes. They should understand the ramifications of violating ethical and professional standards. They must be aware and knowledgeable of non-discrimination laws and policies.

In keeping with professional standards, counselors must have a deep knowledge of relevant agency policy and protocols. They must be able to identify needs for clinical or technical assistance and understand models of clinical and administrative supervision; to make the most of supervision, they should understand and recognize interpersonal dynamics in a supervisory relationship. They must be able to identify personal strengths and weaknesses in the professional setting; in short, they must know when to ask for help. Furthermore, they should understand the rationale for using consultation. Counselors must know the appropriate methods for case presentation.

Ongoing professional development is key for a counselor to maintain the highest professional standards in the field; counselors should therefore recognize the rationale for regular assessment of professional skills and development. They must know the requirements for maintaining their professional credentials and updating them. To do so, counselors should have a current knowledge of the professional literature on substance use disorders. In addition, counselors must be comfortable with the available information on current trends in addiction and related fields. They should know about and join relevant professional associations and take advantage of resources to promote professional growth and competency.

It is impossible to offer high-quality services without the focus and awareness permitted by good personal health. As such, counselors must understand the rationale and know the techniques for periodic self-assessment regarding physical and mental health. Furthermore, they must understand the professional consequences of failing to maintain physical and mental health. Counselors are required to know about the available resources for maintaining physical and mental health (and to take advantage of them as necessary). Counselors must have a strong knowledge of the relationship between physical and mental health. They should have a knowledge of health promotion strategies.

In working with clients, counselors must understand how individual differences like personality, culture, lifestyle, and other factors influence client behavior. Furthermore, they should understand how these factors impact both the assessment and clients' response to treatment. In addition, counselors must have a knowledge of specific differences found in diverse populations. This includes an understanding of the dynamics of family systems in diverse cultures and lifestyles. Counselors must be aware of client advocacy needs specific to diverse cultures and lifestyles.

It is imperative that counselors know and recognize the signs, symptoms, and patterns of violence against persons. They must also be able to identify the risk factors that relate to a client's potential for harm to self or others. Counselors must have a deep knowledge of the requirements for mandatory reporting and the legal consequences of failure to report.

Professionalism in relationships with clients revolves around defining and setting professional boundaries between the client and the counselor: the counselor must know methods for setting and maintaining these limits. Substance abuse counseling may involve many individual partners; one important step is to differentiate between the professional counselor and peer counselor or Twelve Step sponsor. The professional counselor is knowledgeable about different cultures and various culturally sensitive counseling methods. He or she must know and plan for potential impediments to developing the relationship between the client and counselor. Counselors must also have a strong knowledge of the way client reassignment and termination of the counselor-client relationship can impact both parties.

Finally, the counselor must have a knowledge of counseling and psychological theories such as transference and countertransference, the stages of treatment, and the hierarchy of needs and motivation.

Skills

Professional and ethical counselors must be able to appropriately interpret and apply relevant federal, state, and agency regulations regarding addiction counseling;

furthermore, they must provide treatment services that conform to federal, state, and local regulations. In addition, they must be able to interpret and apply professional, legal, and ethical standards. As such, counselors must be able to make ethical decisions that reflect unique needs and situations.

Counselors must demonstrate ethical and professional behavior at all times. They must remain objective, identifying overt and covert feelings and their impact on the counseling relationship; moreover, they must be able to apply therapeutic strategies to client needs. In all situations, counselors must be able to resolve conflicts. They should also be able to make appropriate case presentations.

It is important that counselors be able to communicate the need for assistance. They must be able to identify those situations in which supervision is appropriate and be able to seek and accept supervisory feedback. Furthermore, counselors must elicit feedback from others and accept constructive criticism. It is important for counselors to communicate feelings and concerns openly and respectfully in the workplace.

Counselors must be able to use consultation and supervision to enhance their professional growth. They should actively engage in self-assessment and know how to use specific assessment tools. Counselors must be able to identify professional progress and limitations and to develop plans for resolution or improvement. Part of this is assessing personal training needs, including selecting and participating in appropriate training programs.

Part of self-assessment and professional development includes carrying out regular self-assessment with regards to physical and mental health. Counselors should know and use prevention measures to guard against burnout, and they should employ stress reduction strategies. This means being able to locate and access resources to support physical and mental health. Counselors model self-care as an effective treatment tool.

Another rubric of professional development is reading and interpreting current professional and research-based literature. Counselors should be able to access, understand, and follow this research in order to apply research findings to their clinical practice. More specifically, they should apply their new skills and professional knowledge to client-specific situations and in clinically appropriate ways.

In maintaining a professional clinical practice, counselors must be able to recognize the importance of individual differences that influence client behavior. Furthermore, they must assess and interpret culturally specific client behaviors and lifestyle. It is important that counselors are able to authentically convey respect for cultural and lifestyle diversity in the therapeutic process.

Attitudes

If counselors hold any personal attitudes or behaviors that may conflict with ethical or professional guidelines, they must be open to changing their perspectives; it is paramount that counselors respect professional and ethical standards. Furthermore, they must value compliance with federal, state and agency regulations regarding ethics, confidentiality, and other issues; counselors must be willing to learn to apply them and appreciate the consequences of violations.

Counselors are responsible for their own personal and professional growth; they must be willing to recognize professional development as a professional and personal responsibility. A professional counselor takes an interest in his or her own knowledge and skills base, engaging in ongoing planning to develop it with the recognition that professional growth is an ongoing, career-long process. Counselors must value and participate in self-evaluation. Part of self-evaluation is remaining aware that one's own perspectives and values in substance abuse counseling and recovery may impact job performance; counselors must remain open-minded to information that may be at odds with their own values in the field. Finally, counselors must be open to adjusting their clinical practice to reflect advances in the field.

Keeping an open-minded attitude extends to interactions in the workplace. Counselors should be prepared to take part in peer and supervisor assessments of their clinical skills and practice. They must be open to constructive criticism as well as positive feedback, willing to recognize their personal and professional strengths, weaknesses, and limitations. Further, counselors must be willing to change their behaviors or approaches as appropriate. Overall, counselors should understand and accept the value of supervision in both clinical and administrative settings.

In clinical practice, diverse factors and differences between individuals influence client behavior: counselors must appreciate these differences, integrating their understanding into their practice. Furthermore counselors must recognize and value cultural and lifestyle diversity, recognizing the life experiences and individual perspectives of clients. Counselors should account for their own biases as relevant towards other cultures and lifestyles, being willing to acknowledge and change them as appropriate.

Finally, counselors must realize the importance of their own physical and mental health, recognizing that they are more effective professionally when physically and mentally fit. They should appreciate their position as role models.

In order to maintain confidentiality when providing counseling to a patient with a substance abuse issue, any information received by the counselor is considered confidential and private. The information cannot be shared with other medical professionals even if they need the information for the further treatment of the patient. In order for the information to be provided to the medical professional, there must be a prior authorization provided by the patient.

Authorization is made when the patient signs a disclosure of records, which is done in the presence of the counselor who is providing the treatment to the patient. With the area of confidentiality regarding ethics, a judgment of privilege for proper administration of justice allows disclosure under certain exceptions. Certain examples of "duty to report" include suspected child abuse, or when the abuse of an adult is suspected to be severe or life-threatening.

Duty to Warn

Duty to warn is a process where the counselor providing treatment to the patient takes steps in order to determine whether serious danger is present. For example, if the patient is being abused physically, the potential of serious abuse must be identified and then reported to the appropriate agency. To assess the situation, the counselor should first talk to the supervisor in charge of the treatment plan to obtain assistance to make the correct decision. After this, the case should be referred to the police, so the potential victim can receive the care they need.

Proper Consent

In order to provide proper consent, the patient must be informed when an outside party needs to disclose information that was provided during counseling sessions. The patient does have the right to refuse the disclosure, but they must provide a written statement as to why they do not want to disclose that information to the other party. In certain cases, the law may be able to override the lack of providing disclosure, and the counselor must provide all information regarding the treatment of the patient. This is generally used when legal issues involve abuse problems or issues within the criminal justice system. In some cases where there is no harm, the judge could subpoena the counselor to provide the information.

In certain situations, verbal communication is not considered to be disclosure of information of the patient. This occurs when information is given to specific agencies such as other mental health facilities providing treatment to the patient.

If confidential counseling information is requested regarding an adolescent, the disclosure of the information is treated in the same way as with an adult. The minor must be informed regarding the request for the information, determine if they want to release information, and then both the parent and the minor must sign a consent form.

There are certain laws and ethical procedures involved with clinical charting, including the counselor's use of documentation in order to make progress notes for the client and on the counseling sessions. In order to correctly follow the legal and ethical concerns regarding documentation of the patient's information, the counselor must provide facts without releasing too much information regarding the treatment process.

Notation Guidelines

- Use black ink because it enables you to make copies that are easy to read.

- Take time to create notes that are easy to read. A logical, well written document will have a clear pattern, appropriate paragraphs, and good grammar. Some notes may be typed in order to provide the most clearly written information. By taking this step, you could reduce misunderstanding of the notes and avoid adverse effects.

- Different agencies use different note formats. These are formed during note writing, and the note writing format used by the agency should be used at all times by the counselor.

- While choosing words, it is important that the worst issues are documented carefully, and the emphasis is placed on important areas, such as when the patient had made statements or reports.

- Use enough information with envelopes so that the concept of the session can be captured. However, avoid excessive note-taking.

- While creating the notes, take into consideration the future readers, such as healthcare providers, court reporters, or legal professionals.

Documentation

Proper documentation involves recording the screening and intake process, assessment, treatment plan, clinical reports, clinical progress notes, discharge summaries, and other client-related data.

These include, but are not limited to: psychoactive substance use and abuse history, physical health, psychological information, social information, history of criminality, spiritual information, recreational information, nutritional information, educational and/or vocational information, sexual information, and legal information.

The Discharge Summary

A discharge summary should include a profile of the client, with relevant demographic information; the client's presenting symptoms and diagnoses; any relevant interventions; any critical incidents during treatment; information on the client's progress toward positive treatment objectives; outcomes; the client's aftercare plan; the client's prognosis; and relevant recommendations.

Knowledge

Record-management is key in writing a discharge summary, and so counselors must have a deep knowledge of the basic elements of client records such as release forms, assessments, treatment plans, progress notes, and discharge plans. Counselors also require a strong knowledge of current regulations applicable to client records, including program, state, and federal confidentiality regulations and laws and how to apply them. In addition, they should specifically understand the confidentiality requirements pertaining to infectious diseases. It is essential that counselors understand records as legal documents. Finally, counselors should know the proper procedures for reviewing and updating records.

Appropriate record management means using the proper clinical terminology to explain client progress; therefore, counselors should be comfortable with this vocabulary and terminology. They must understand the accepted measures for determining the treatment outcomes, including methods of gathering data, and be aware of related research defining treatment outcomes. Moreover, they must understand the principles supporting the use of outcome data in order to evaluate treatment programs. Finally, counselors must be able to distinguish between evaluations of process and outcome.

In general, counselors should have a strong knowledge of current federal, state, local, and program regulations, as well as regulations pertaining to informed consent.

Skills

Here, counselors require strong writing skills. They must produce client records by compiling them in a timely, clear and concise fashion, using new technologies as appropriate and in accordance with regulations. Information should always be documented objectively, clearly and, if handwritten, legibly.

In general, important skills for counselors here are the ability to analyze, synthesize, and summarize information. Thus, counselors must be able to identify and concisely record information that is relevant. Furthermore, they must have a firm grasp of clinical technology and know how to use it correctly and appropriately. Counselors must be able to collect and record outcome data, and they must be able to integrate outcome measures throughout the treatment process in order to gauge progress, reporting measurable results. Counselors are responsible for recording any changes in the client's treatment plan. They also produce clear and concise discharge summaries.

Above all, counselors must be able to apply federal, state, and agency confidentiality regulations to documentation management (including those regulations applicable to infectious diseases as relevant for addiction treatment). This includes explaining client rights and protecting them, as well as explaining regulations not only to clients but also to third parties. When appropriate, counselors request, prepare, and complete release of information in accordance with relevant regulations. Professional management of documentation includes ensuring the security of clinical records, in both their physical and digital forms.

Attitudes

In clinical charting, counselors must value accurate documentation and be motivated to produce accurate reports. Counselors should appreciate that prompt recording is essential for accuracy. Furthermore, they must embrace the need for objectivity in reporting client progress. It is essential to record plans for both treatment and continuing care; counselors should appreciate this need. As part of their commitment to professionalism, counselors must respect the need for supervision as needed to understand and properly apply confidentiality regulations. Clients have rights to privacy and confidentiality, and a professional counselor honors these rights; thus, counselors must appreciate the absolute necessity of safeguarding records.

Documentation and accurate records are important because treatment is a process and recovery is an ongoing, dynamic element in the life of a recovering addict. Therefore, accurate and up-to-date data permits regular evaluation of client progress throughout the course of treatment, and it enables ongoing improvement of clinical practice.

Ethics & Counselor Responsibilities

Students in practicum must behave in accordance with the Ethical Standards of the American Counseling Association. Practicum permits students to put ethical standards into practice when working with private client information, obtaining informed consent and authorization for audio and video recording, and protecting client anonymity.

Students must practice refraining from specifying client names and recording other information that could reveal a client's identity. They must learn to obtain written permission (the client's signature) before recording; in the case of minors, counselors must obtain consent from their parents or guardians. The practicum student should be cautious to obtain appropriate consultation when instances occur outside of his or her range of competency.

CACREP Vision and Mission

The overall goal of practicum is for the student counselor to gain experience, integrate past learning experiences, develop competencies, increase self-awareness, and gain insight into theory and technique. As an accrediting body, the Counseling for the Accreditation of Counseling and Related Educational Programs (CACREP) develops standards and procedures that reflect the needs of a complex and diverse society. It supports and promotes high-quality, accredited preparation programs to develop the skills and professionalism of counselors and related professionals so that they can offer optimal services to clients.

CACREP Clinical Mental Health Counseling Practicum Standards

The participant should demonstrate the following, in accordance with accepted, effective, and appropriate strategies:

- Abides by ethical and legal standards in clinical mental health counseling.

- In initiation, maintenance, and termination of counseling, practices diagnosis, treatment, referral, and prevention of mental and emotional disorders.

- Utilizes multicultural competencies in clinical mental health counseling.

- Assists clients in understanding and accessing community resources.

- In initiation, maintenance, and termination of counseling, utilizes those modalities appropriate for the specific culture of the individual, couple, family, group, and/or system.

- Able to assess and manage suicide risk in accordance with appropriate procedures.

- Follows record-keeping standards applicable to clinical mental health counseling.

- Utilizes those strategies specifically applicable to clients with addiction and co-occurring disorders as appropriate.

- Recognizes his or her own professional limitations and is willing to seek supervision or refer clients as necessary.

- Makes referrals as appropriate using current information about local resources and keeping information up-to-date.

- Tailors counseling systems, theories, techniques, and interventions to ensure they are culturally appropriate for various populations.

- To plan treatment and manage caseloads, effectively conducts an intake interview, a mental status evaluation, a biopsychosocial history, a mental health history, and a psychological assessment.

- Able to appropriately screen for addiction, aggression danger to self and/or others, and co-occurring mental disorders.

- Able to draw inferences from assessment information in evaluating individual students and the effectiveness of educational programs.

- Assesses obstacles to students' academic, professional, and personal development.

- Collaborates with parents, guardians, and families to address problems affecting student success in school.

- Identifies community resources for use in the school to improve student achievement and success.

- Collaborates with teachers, staff, and community organizations to promote student academic, career, and personal/social development.

- Obtains assistance for students and their families through referral procedures.

Practice Examination

1. **To understand addiction, the counselor must comprehend which aspects of addiction?**

A. Social

B. Economic

C. Cultural

D. All of the above

2. **According to researchers, the concept of addiction something caused by:**

A. The mood of the patient.

B. The psychological state of the patient.

C. The physical state of the patient.

D. All of the above

3. **What should be used to evaluate and assess the patient's addiction?**

A. Biomarkers

B. Laboratory testing

C. Patient's own report of substance use

D. Counselor's opinion of substance use

4. **The elements involved in the psychological aspect of addiction include all of the following EXCEPT:**

A. Sense of powerlessness

B. Sense of hopelessness

C. Sense of rage

D. Sense of accomplishment

5.   **What is the term for using a drug in a manner or for a reason that differs from how it was prescribed, which is often unintentional?**

A. Misuse

B. Abuse

C. Dependence

D. Tolerance

6.   **Physical dependence occurs when:**

A. Drug or alcohol abuse has occurred for a prolonged period, and the person can become both mentally and physically addicted to the drug.

B. A person has a strong mental urge to use a drug to experience the effects considered to be pleasant (drug or alcohol used to reach a euphoric state of mind).

C. A person may use another drug form to lessen the withdrawal they are experiencing from their drug of choice.

D. A person's body is used to taking the drug, and they start to experience withdrawal symptoms when the drug is no longer present in their system.

7.   **The amount of time the drug stays present within the body is called the:**

A. Dose

B. Half-life

C. Lethal dose

D. Therapeutic dose

8.   **Drug interactions can occur between:**

A. Street drugs

B. Prescription drugs

C. Alcohol

D. All of the above

9. Using a drug in a manner other than that prescribed, with the intention of getting high, is called:

A. Use

B. Misuse

C. Abuse

D. Dependence

10. This can cause a person to become more sensitive to the drug over a period of time:

A. Physical dependence

B. Tolerance

C. Abuse

D. Reverse tolerance

11. Regarding drug administration, what is considered to be the most rapid method of action for a substance?

A. Oral

B. Intravenous

C. Injection

D. Snorting (intranasal)

12. What is a danger of intranasal (snorting) drug administration?

A. Severe damage to the sinus cavity

B. Brain damage

C. Both A and B

D. Neither A nor B

13. **What can occur if a time-release medication is crushed or the capsule is opened so the components can be taken?**

A. Too little of the medication will be provided during one period of time.

B. Too much of the medication will be provided during one period of time.

C. Both A and B

D. Neither A nor B

14. **Why would someone desire to use cocaine in a suppository or rectal form?**

A. The mucus membranes in the rectum area can absorb some drugs quickly.

B. The nerve endings in the rectum area can absorb some drugs quickly.

C. The mucus membranes in the rectum area make the drug more potent.

D. The nerve endings in the rectum make the drug more potent.

15. **These types of injections are done by injecting the drug of choice into the soft tissue present under the skin:**

A. Intramuscular

B. Intravenous

C. Intradermal

D. Subcutaneous

16. **What types of drug requires eating or drinking for administration?**

A. Certain types of mushrooms

B. LSD

C. Alcohol

D. All of the above

17. Infections can occur during injection drug administration due to:

A. Use of cotton that gets stuck within the syringe.

B. Lack of proper preparation.

C. An unsterile injection site.

D. All of the above

18. Regarding toxicology testing, when should urine testing be done?

A. Within two days of the drug use

B. Within three days of the drug use

C. Within four days of the drug use

D. Within five days of the drug use

19. Which type of toxicology testing is the most effective for drugs?

A. Blood testing

B. Saliva testing

C. Hair testing

D. Urine testing

20. This type of toxicology testing is done by using the swab on the inside of the cheek, and then enclosing the swab in a sterilized container that will be sent to a lab for testing:

A. Swab testing

B. Saliva testing

C. Cheek testing

D. Container testing

21. **How many drugs can be assessed with blood toxicology testing?**

A. Up to three

B. Up to five

C. Up to fifteen

D. Up to thirty

22. **The toxicology testing method depends upon:**

A. The patient's report of use

B. The reason for testing

C. The counselor's preference

D. All of the above

23. **Signs of addiction with impairment include all of the following EXCEPT:**

A. Inability to keep a job or attend school

B. Use of substances in high risk situations, such as while driving

C. Legal consequences due to use of drugs

D. Having depression due to alcohol or substance use

24. **Which of the following does NOT play a role in biological addiction?**

A. Tolerance

B. Genetics

C. Biochemistry

D. Metabolism

25.   What enzyme is thought to play a role in the susceptibility to alcohol abuse due to genetic disposition?

A. BYOB

B. MYOB

C. CYOB

D. DYOB

26.   According to research studies, people with severe mental illnesses only experience success with recovery:

A. 10 percent of the time

B. 20 percent of the time

C. 35 percent of the time

D. 50 percent of the time

27.   The addiction advocacy movement was created in order to provide recovery to patients by:

A. Involving the interdisciplinary team

B. Involving the patient's significant other

C. Involving the counselor

D. Involving the patient's family

28.   The concept of recovery in addiction is:

A. A plan that works by implementing a treatment program that provides transformational change in those who are going through the process of recovery.

B. A plan that works by assessing the patient for transformational change while going through the process of recovery.

C. A plan that works by implementing an outpatient program that provides knowledge of addiction.

D. None of the above

29. Regarding substance abuse education and treatment, who could benefit from primary prevention measures?

A. Adolescents

B. Young people

C. Individuals with little or no history of drug and/or alcohol abuse.

D. All of the above

30. Which of the following is NOT one of the primary prevention measures?

A. Promoting abstinence from drugs and alcohol.

B. Teaching refusal skills to those who haven't used.

C. Decreasing the age of usage, such as age limit to buy alcohol.

D. Providing education on the dangers associated with drugs and alcohol use.

31. Reducing the available supply of drugs and alcohol through appropriate measures, including legal assistance, is a form of:

A. Recovery

B. Prevention

C. Treatment

D. Assessment

32. Providing education on the risks, dangers, and other negative factors associated with use and abuse is an example of:

A. Primary prevention

B. Secondary prevention

C. Tertiary prevention

D. All of the above

33. The counselor uses a specialized approach to treatment that includes desensitizing users to triggers, such as people, places, things, and actions. What type of prevention is this?

A. Primary prevention

B. Secondary prevention

C. Tertiary prevention

D. Quaternary prevention

34. The counselor teaches the 12 step principles to the patient in order to prepare him or her for leaving treatment after completion. What form of prevention is this?

A. Primary prevention

B. Secondary prevention

C. Tertiary prevention

D. Quaternary prevention

35. This process involves meeting with the family and significant others of the addict:

A. Intervention

B. Cooperation

C. Location

D. Direction

36. This person uses substances heavily, but hasn't seen negative effects occur in health or life:

A. Moderate and non-problematic user

B. Heavy and non-problematic user

C. Heavy user with moderate problems

D. Heavy user with serious problems

37. The correct order for the steps for treating addiction is:

A. Assess, identify, stabilize, rehabilitate

B. Identify, stabilize, rehabilitate, assess

C. Identify, assess, stabilize, rehabilitate

D. Stabilize, assess, rehabilitate, identify

38. This rehabilitation program is typically used for patients that have successfully completed an inpatient or outpatient rehab program:

A. Co-occurring treatment program

B. Aftercare program

C. Intense care program

D. Self-help program

39. This program is a fellowship for families who are not addicts, but who have one in their family, and members are trying to understand the addiction and how they can manage their own lives:

A. Al-Anon

B. Alcoholics Anonymous

C. Al-Teen

D. Al-Alc

40. HIV:

A. Has the fastest transition rate among all STDs.

B. Is most common among those who use drugs in the form of administering them with syringe for injection.

C. Is a growing epidemic among IV drug users.

D. All of the above

41. Which of the following is NOT one of the modes of HIV transmission?

A. Vaginal intercourse

B. Anal intercourse

C. Sharing needles

D. Sharing hairbrushes

42. Of the following, which is NOT a sign that a recovering addict is ready for vocational rehabilitation?

A. She shows ongoing sobriety.

B. She understands why vocational rehabilitation is needed.

C. She recognizes that substance use is likely to recur.

D. She addresses entry issues as part of a better life goal plan.

43. The counselor assists the patient in learning he has much to offer in terms of helping others, as this will boost self-esteem. What therapeutic technique is this?

A. Bonding

B. Creating hope

C. Education

D. Altruism

44. The counselor wants to use a therapeutic technique for expression. What should he do?

A. Discuss events and feelings as the main focus of the group.

B. Encourage members of group to reconnect with important people in their life who were lost due to the addiction, such as close friends and family members.

C. Help members to listen and take part in different group activities in order to improve or reconnect with their social skills, such as taking part in role playing activities.

D. Group members will have deep fears and hidden feelings arise during the discussions, which will allow these issues to be addressed and worked through.

45.   **The first step for immediate crisis intervention is:**

A. Provide support to the recovering addict.

B. Initiate an intervention.

C. Offer hope with positive statements.

D. Provide a solution to the problem.

46.   **The counselor puts himself in the patient's shoes in order to develop understanding of addiction and related problems. What is this technique?**

A. Reflection

B. Active listening

C. Empathy

D. Paraphrasing

47.   **In order to encourage the patient to explain things in further detail, the counselor should:**

A. Use reflection

B. Use cues

C. Use open-ended questions

D. Use summarization

48.   **This type of therapy uses different methods to encourage the patient to take part in activities designed to change overall patterns of thinking, behavior, and methods of handling issues faced throughout the recovery process:**

A. Cognitive therapy

B. Talk therapy

C. Hypnosis therapy

D. Psychoanalysis

49.   The counselor determines reasons why a family is dysfunctional, examines problems and figures out a solution for better family dynamics. What type of counseling technique is used here?

A. Education

B. Joining

C. Structured analysis

D. All of the above

50.   Which is a true statement concerning domestic abuse battering?

A. Battering is secondary to a mental disorder.

B. Battering is only caused by substance use and abuse.

C. Battering is done because the perpetrator suffers from low self-esteem.

D. Battering is caused by loss of emotion.

51.   This treatment technique for domestic violence is used as a process to determine how each person within the relationship views abuse:

A. Funneling

B. Interviewing

C. Emotional expression

D. Assertiveness

52.   During which stage of the cycle of abuse does the abuser often become apologetic?

A. Stage 1

B. Stage 2

C. Stage 3

D. Stage 4

53. If an individual believes that abstinence is too difficult to achieve or maintain, and uses substances as a result, which of the following has taken place?

A. Abstinence violation effect (AVE)

B. Substance reuse effect (SRE)

C. Abstinence reuse effect (ARE)

D. Substance violation effect (SVE)

54. One very common trait among addicts of all backgrounds is:

A. A complete lack of money

B. A complete lack of family

C. A complete lack of spirituality

D. A complete lack of direction

55. When providing addiction treatment, the counselor should:

A. Avoid pushing the patient into spiritual beliefs during the treatment process.

B. Refer the patient to spiritual groups if he or she chooses to take that approach.

C. Allow the patient to guide conversations about spirituality.

D. All of the above

56. Change can be observed in the addict by all of the following EXCEPT:

A. The patient will take part in interconnected change and self-discovery.

B. The patient will continue to have doubts throughout the entire recovery process.

C. The patient will develop an action plan that he or she will use during all times of the recovery.

D. The patient will maintain hope throughout the recovery process by using positive coping skills that he or she has developed.

57.   During which stage of change does the patient plan to make a change, even if he or she has failed recently or in the past?

A. Stage 1 - Precontemplation

B. Stage 2 - Preparation

C. Stage 3 - Action

D. Stage 4 - Maintenance

58.   During this stage, major changes are made, and relaxation is no longer an issue for the patient, as he or she continues to be active in recovery:

A. Stage 1 - Precontemplation

B. Stage 2 - Action

C. Stage 4 - Maintenance

D. Stage 5 - Termination

59.   How many phases of motivational counseling are there?

A. 3

B. 4

C. 5

D. 6

60.   The counselor works with the patient in order to help him develop love and trust in himself. By developing this, the patient is creating external and internal support. What type of motivational counseling is this?

A. Empathy

B. Discrepancy

C. Resistance

D. None of the above

61. When both substance abuse and a mental disorder are present, they are considered a:

A. Dual addictive disorder

B. Dual diagnosis

C. Double addiction

D. Double diagnosis

62. Which configuration style is a less forceful approach to recovery, and may offer better results for some patients?

A. Gentle approach

B. Multiple intervention approach

C. Unique approach

D. Addiction approach

63. The New Beginnings Center provides a wide range of therapy services and helps to implement the services into the patient's everyday life. This therapy includes job assistance, skills building, and other valuable resources. What type of treatment model does this rehabilitation center use?

A. Assertive Community Therapy Model

B. Broker Generalist Model

C. Process Treatment Model

D. Strategy-Based Model

64. The Primary Treatment Assessment Process involves all of these EXCEPT:

A. Detecting special skills or defects within the patient

B. Providing basic supplemental needs to the patient

C. Identifying the level of regular ability to function with the patient

D. Detecting various patient success strategies

65. **Decisions made by a counselor in a manner that regards the patient's best interest are considered:**

A. Ethics decisions

B. Moral decisions

C. Truthful decisions

D. Professional decisions

66. **A set of principles that create moral decisions involving patient care and value are:**

A. Moral principles

B. Rules and regulation principles

C. Ethical principles

D. Law principles

67. **What does a patient have to sign in order to share confidential counseling records with another mental health facility?**

A. A disclosure of ethics

B. A disclosure of records

C. A prior authorization

D. An information authorization

68. **A process where a counselor needs to take steps in order to determine whether serious danger is present is called:**

A. Duty to warn

B. Duty to disclose

C. Authorization to warn

D. Authorization to disclose

69. What aspect of pharmacology determines the level of addiction in a person?

A. The strength of the drug

B. The person's gender

C. The method of administration

D. All of the above

70. A substance prescribed to a patient to treat a condition, which may have a potential for abuse, is called:

A. A substance

B. A drug

C. A medicine

D. All of the above

71. A state that occurs when drug or alcohol abuse has occurred for a prolonged period of time is:

A. Misuse

B. Dependence

C. Psychological dependence

D. Reverse dependence

72. When a person uses another drug form to lessen the withdrawal they are experiencing from their drug of choice, it is called:

A. Dependence

B. Abuse

C. Cross-dependence

D. Reverse dependence

73. This causes a person to become more sensitive to a drug over a period of time, rather than less sensitive:

A. Tolerance

B. Reverse tolerance

C. Psychological dependence

D. Physical dependence

74. The amount of drug needed by the person in order for it to be effective is called:

A. The lethal dose

B. The half-life dose

C. The therapeutic dose

D. The maximum dose

75. What type of risk exists with intravenous drug use?

A. The risk of infection

B. The risk of overdose

C. The risk of addiction

D. All of the above

76. What is the street name for a fungal substance that grows naturally in certain regions of the world and gives euphoria when eaten?

A. "Shrooms"

B. "Acid"

C. "Buttons"

D. "DMT"

77.   When a urine drug test is sent to the laboratory, this can:

A. Provide faster results

B. Provide sterile results

C. Provide more accurate results

D. All of the above

78.   How is saliva testing done?

A. The patient spits some saliva in a cup, which is sent to the laboratory.

B. The patient coughs up some saliva, and puts into a test tube.

C. A swab made from cotton material is used to take a sample of the saliva on the inside of the cheek, and then the swab is enclosed in a sterilized container that will be sent to a lab for testing.

D. A syringe made from plastic used to take a sample of the saliva on the inside of the cheek, and then the syringe is enclosed in a sterilized container that will be sent to a lab for testing.

79.   Regardless of the amount or number of drugs being assessed, when conducting blood toxicology testing, how many samples or vials are required?

A. 1

B. 2

C. 3

D. 4

80.   If a person has many fights and altercations, and eventually suffers from a car accident, this is a sign of:

A. Impairment due to substance use

B. Casual use of a substance

C. Normal behavior for a young person

D. None of the above

81.   Who would have a lower tolerance to alcohol?

A. A 155-pound woman

B. A 275-pound man

C. A 125-pound man

D. A 132-pound woman

82.   Signs of genetic factors associated with addiction in a young person include all of the following EXCEPT:

A. Bubbly personality

B. Lack of social skills

C. Violent behaviors

D. Impulsive behaviors

83.   When providing counseling and treatment for a recovering addict, the counselor should provide several levels of care. Which of the following would NOT be an appropriate type of therapy?

A. Family therapy

B. Group therapy

C. Individual therapy

D. Cultural therapy

84.   For those going through recovery, the concept of recovery in addiction is a plan that works by implementing a treatment program that provides:

A. Transformational change

B. Temporary change

C. Immediate change

D. Permanent change

85.   The chance of a successful recovery from addiction is increased when:

A. Therapy is used to help the patient gain new skills.

B. The patient's mental health issue is treated.

C. The patient's physical health issue is treated.

D. Genetic factors are addressed.

86.   A group of individuals are working together in order to provide education on drug use to a group of young African American adolescents. What is this group called?

A. A prevention group

B. A treatment group

C. A rehab group

D. An intervention group

87.   The main goal of a prevention group is:

A. To offer treatment to at-risk youths

B. To offer a safe house to at-risk youths

C. To stop drug use from occurring

D. To stop the transmission of HIV

88.   A group of individuals reduces the amount of demand present for drugs and alcohol by providing those in the community with appropriate treatment methods. This is an example of:

A. Rehabilitation

B. Prevention

C. Treatment

D. Community service

89.   A youth organization is promoting safe alternatives by offering community activities to schoolchildren and providing education regarding the dangers associated with drug and alcohol use. This is an example of:

A. Primary prevention

B. Secondary prevention

C. Tertiary prevention

D. Quaternary prevention

90.   The term "referral" means:

A. Meeting other counselors for discussions regarding patients

B. Assisting a patient with using support services and available resources

C. Providing alcohol and drug education to patients

D. Attending an NA, AA, or Al-Anon meeting with the patient

91.   What is the counselor most concerned with during a crisis interview with a patient?

A. Getting all the pertinent information possible

B. What the immediate response should be

C. The patient's family dynamics and available support systems

D. Focusing questions on the present situation and the patient's coping skills

92. A single mother with four children comes into the clinic where you work. When discussing her current drug use, she tells you she has not been back to the apartment for three days, but left her 10-year-old son in charge. What should you do?

A. Admit her for immediate treatment and arrange for childcare.

B. Contact child protective services to report this.

C. Call law enforcement to have her arrested for child neglect.

D. Send her home to make arrangements for childcare before returning for treatment.

93. A patient is showing signs of denial due to discrepancies he makes during the intake interview. Which one of the following statements should the counselor make that would be MOST appropriate?

A. "You have told me several different things. Which one is the truth?"

B. "I am not sure I understand you, so please clarify this."

C. "Denial is part of addiction."

D. "Your story is quite confusing."

94. One tertiary prevention measure a treatment center could use is:

A. Using pharmaceutical approaches

B. Admitting the patient to a homeless shelter

C. Exposing the addict to triggers

D. Educating the patient on prevention of STDs

95. The intervention process is successful when applied using the correct measures of:

A. Attached caring

B. Detached caring

C. Recovery

D. Healing

96.   One of the benefits of intervention is that it stops denial of the addiction in:

A. The addict

B. The family members

C. Significant others

D. All of the above

97.   A person who uses drugs often and has had a few issues occur as a result of the use is considered a/an:

A. Heavy and non-problematic user

B. Heavy user with serious problems

C. Heavy user with moderate problems

D. Moderate and non-problematic user

98.   This person is unable to stop drugs due to physical and mental addiction. Also, the use and abuse of substances has caused issues in the patient's personal life, as well has had a negative effect on their health:

A. Heavy user with serious problems

B. Heavy user with moderate problems

C. Dependent and addicted with life and health problems

D. Dependent and addicted with health problems

99.   During this treatment step, the counselor helps the addict stop use of the drug through detox and the use of pharmaceutical alternatives:

A. Step 1 - Identify

B. Step 2 - Assessment

C. Step 3 - Stabilize

D. Step 4 - Rehabilitate

100. The counselor determines the proper long-term treatment program for the patient based upon the issues detected during the assessment and development of overall treatment plan. What treatment step is this?

A. Step 1 - Identify

B. Step 2 - Assessment

C. Step 3 - Stabilize

D. Step 4 - Rehabilitate

101. Rehab centers that offer the same type of care as inpatient rehabilitation facilities, except the patient leaves the facility and goes home after the treatment is completed each day, are called:

A. Co-occurring treatment centers

B. Day treatment centers

C. Aftercare treatment centers

D. Outpatient treatment centers

102. Of the following statements about goal setting for the treatment of addiction, which is NOT true?

A. Goal setting is an important part of the treatment program

B. Goals are based on the counselor's desires

C. Goals are based on the patient's desires

D. Goals are created using realistic measures

103. Which of the following is NOT a benefit of goal setting for the recovering addict:

A. Makes is easier for the patient to achieve sobriety

B. The patient reviews goals regularly to keep perspective

C. Helps the patient stay on track

D. Gives the patient success stories to share with others

104. This type of therapy gives the patient the opportunity to relate to others who are going through similar issues:

A. Individual therapy

B. Couples therapy

C. Group therapy

D. Family therapy

105. The Twelve Step approach was created as the original principle for:

A. Alcoholics Anonymous

B. Group therapy

C. Individual counseling

D. Family therapy

106. Narcotics Anonymous

A. Does not recognize alcohol as a drug.

B. Does not recognize habit-forming prescription medications as drugs.

C. Is open to addicts regardless of their drug of choice (including alcohol).

D. Is not a Twelve Step program.

107. Working the Twelve Steps includes

A. Working with other people in recovery.

B. Spending time in isolation.

C. Choosing in what order to work the steps.

D. The right to ignore the principles of the Twelve Steps.

108. A Twelve Step program:

A. Is a self-help program.

B. Is based on certain principles.

C. Requires peer support.

D. All of the above.

109. Who regulates the universal precautions and guidelines?

A. Occupational Safety and Health Administration (OSHA)

B. Centers for Disease Control and Prevention (CDC)

C. American Medical Association (AMA)

D. American Drug Council (ADC)

110. HIV is a virus that is contagious and can be spread via:

A. Urine

B. Physical contact

C. Airborne transmission

D. Blood and body fluids

111. This disease has the fastest transition rate among all STDs:

A. Hepatitis B Virus (HBV)

B. Hepatitis A Virus (HAV)

C. Human Immunodeficiency Virus (HIV)

D. Influenza Virus

112.   One way HIV is transmitted in social groups is:

A. When group members share eating utensils

B. When members engage in unprotected sexual activity with multiple other members of the group

C. When group members share sleeping bags and bed linens

D. All of the above

113.   What happens when the HIV virus is exposed to air?

A. It will die.

B. It lives for five minutes and then will die.

C. It lives for ten minutes and then will die.

D. It lives for thirty minutes and then will die.

114.   HIV transmission is more likely when:

A. The person is younger than sixteen years.

B. The person is a female.

C. The person has recently been infected.

D. The person is taking antiretroviral drugs.

115.   What is the purpose of providing treatment for someone who has HIV?

A. It can be cured.

B. HIV can be suppressed for many years, and HIV positive people can live normal, healthy lives.

C. The virus can be suppressed for two years.

D. There is no reason to give treatment because it will progress to AIDS.

116.   Of the following symptoms, which is NOT one that is related to HIV?

A. Flu-like symptoms

B. Fevers

C. Fatigue

D. Hearing loss

117.   Why is sexual intercourse such a risky behavior for those who have drug addictions?

A. Sex is often offered in exchange for drugs when addiction has progressed.

B. Being intoxicated makes engaging in unprotected sex more likely.

C. Oral sex can lead to herpes.

D. All of the above

118.   The process of risk reduction counseling involves using substance-abuse prevention in order to:

A. Educate addicts on problems with addiction

B. Stop the spread of STDs

C. Stop the spread of pneumonia

D. Offer counseling sessions

119.   How can a counselor help the addict when he or she is actively using drugs intravenously?

A. Discuss self-exams to detect issues regarding health

B. Give information on changes that help build the immune system

C. Provide the patient with information on the steps he or she needs to take for a rapid and healthy lifestyle changes

D. All of the above

120. The counselor can offer external resources to the recovering addict. Which of the following is NOT considered appropriate?

A. Housesitting

B. Home healthcare

C. Support groups

D. Personal friendships

121. The counselor is working with a recovering addict who is HIV positive. He tells the patient there is hope for a successful recovery. The counselor wants to instill hope for the patient because when a patient feels that there is no hope for their future, it can cause:

A. Major depression

B. Anxiety

C. Serious physical illness

D. Relapse

122. Caseworkers and counselors should give pre-infection advice when dealing with addicts and persons in recovery. These professionals should ensure that the treatment is one aimed towards:

A. Recovery from drugs and alcohol

B. Prevention of STDs

C. Both recovery from drug and alcohol use and prevention of STDs

D. Proper education regarding well-being

123. User training, knowledge, and skills regarding STDs help with educating the recovering addict regarding the transmission of STDs. To apply this in a group setting, or in a one-on-one setting, the counselor will need to:

A. Follow the instruction manual

B. Gain experience

C. Train in a classroom setting

D. Train alongside experienced mentors

124. The counselor uses a therapeutic technique to connect with the patient so that he does not feel alone. What is this called?

A. Creating hope

B. Altruism

C. Bonding

D. Education

125. The counselor helps a group member to listen and take part in different group activities in order to improve or reconnect with their social skills, such as taking part in role playing activities. What is this therapeutic technique?

A. Resolving conflicts

B. Initiating lost connections

C. Copying actions

D. Developing social skills

126. Group members will have deep fears and hidden feelings arise during the discussions. What is this called?

A. Subconscious feelings

B. Copying actions

C. Personal development

D. Trust for others

127. Allowing recovering addicts to learn how to express negative feelings to others in a manner that leads to resolutions is called:

A. Developing trust for own feelings

B. Developing appropriate confrontational techniques

C. Developing trust for others

D. Developing behavior plan changes

128. Why is it important for a recovering addict to develop a behavior plan for change?

A. By expressing emotions and seeing the same emotions within group members, the recovering addict will begin to develop a plan to change negative behavior patterns

B. By expressing anger with group members, the recovering addict will begin to recognize positive behavior patterns and develop a plan to maintain them

C. By expressing emotions, discussing them and getting positive feedback, the members will be able to recognize and trust their own feelings more

D. By discussing emotions to group members, the patient will gain trust for others

129. All of the following are benefits of crisis intervention and resolution EXCEPT:

A. Create a helping resolution with the patient

B. Secure a safe environment for the patient

C. Offer support to the patient's family

D. Help the patient create a plan for action during times of distress

130. This form of treatment can offer the recovering addict the ability to express deep issues and concerns that he or she may not feel comfortable with expressing within a group setting:

A. Psychoanalysis

B. Individual counseling

C. Hypnosis

D. Family therapy

131. Which of the following occurs when individual counseling occurs along with group therapy?

A. The recovering addict will relapse

B. The recovering addict will completely recover

C. The recovering addict will have a better chance at recovery

D. None of the above

132. The counselor repeats important information given by a patient so that he or she can hear what was said and reflect on it. What counseling technique is this?

A. Coping skills

B. Paraphrasing

C. Empathy

D. Active listening

133. Taking complex issues the patient is facing and offering simple solutions that can be used to resolve the conflict is called:

A. Offering simplicity

B. Offering complexity

C. Using cues

D. Using reflection

134. This form of treatment creates a secure and effective environment where the patient can discuss his or her issues in confidence, and the therapist can offer encouragement, support, and positive coping techniques:

A. Cognitive therapy

B. Open therapy

C. Talk therapy

D. Communication therapy

135.   Individual counseling is usually:

A. Short-term

B. Long-term

C. Both A and B

D. Neither A nor B

136.   Family members of a recovering addict can take part in:

A. Use and abuse of substances

B. Overuse of substances

C. Enabling the addict

D. All of the above

137.   To assist with family members of the recovering addict, the counselor can offer:

A. Coping techniques

B. Work opportunities

C. Referrals

D. Social services

138.   When the counselor determines reasons for a family's dysfunction, examines problems, and figures out a solution for better family dynamics, he or she is using:

A. Joining

B. Education

C. Structured analysis

D. Alternative coping techniques

139.   The use of a methadone program is considered:

A. Drug use

B. Drug substitution

C. Drug rehabilitation

D. Relapse prevention

140.   Many women who are subjected to abuse:

A. Go to a shelter to cope with the abuse.

B. Turn to friends to cope with the abuse.

C. Use drugs to cope with the abuse.

D. Use distraction to cope with the abuse.

141.   With cases involving domestic violence, when the counselor encourages the addict to stop blaming the use of a substance for the cause of the battery, this technique is called:

A. Funneling

B. Emotional expression

C. Eliminating blame

D. Analyzing abuse

142.   All of the following are issues seen with children who are part of a household involving addiction EXCEPT:

A. Lack of feelings

B. Self-harm

C. Enhanced self-worth

D. Boundary issues

143. When counseling an adolescent who lives with an addict, the counselor should determine how both the adolescent and the user may play a role within that addiction process. It is important to tell the adolescent:

A. That addiction is a disease

B. That he or she is not responsible for the addiction

C. That enabling is not likely to occur

D. That the situation will get better

144. Concerning family counseling, a continued denial of the addiction will lead to:

A. Short-term negative effects for the addict

B. Long-term negative effects for the addict

C. Short-term negative effects for the entire family

D. Long-term negative effects for the entire family

145. Assessment of the addict and the substance use/abuse involves the collection of data from the individual, as well as corroborative sources. This is done to:

A. Determine the extent of the addiction

B. Determine the addict's strengths

C. Formulate a plan of treatment

D. All of the above

146. Substance abuse and associated treatment services should be:

A. Standardized

B. Mandatory

C. Regulated

D. Individualized

147. During inpatient treatment, what should be used to ensure that the patient receives all necessary services in a timely and coordinated manner?

A. An intense plan

B. A case manager

C. An educated counselor

D. A psychologist

148. Recovery and relapse are:

A. Ongoing processes

B. Terminal processes

C. Short-term events

D. Intermediate events

149. Abstinence violation effect refers to:

A. What happens when a person fails to abstain from a negative habitual behavior

B. What happens when a person attempts to maintain a positive habitual behavior

C. What happens when a person fails to maintain sobriety

D. What happens when a person successfully maintains sobriety

150. The Type One Professional Experience Questionnaire examines:

A. Psychological and behavioral issues involved in the addiction process

B. Psychological issues involved in the addiction process

C. Spiritual issues involved in the addiction process

D. Behavioral issue involved in the addiction process

Answers and Explanations

1.   Answer: D. All of the above

Explanation: The counselor must understand the social, economic, and cultural aspects of addiction.

2.   Answer: B. The psychological state of the patient.

Explanation: According to researchers, the concept of addiction is known to be something caused by the psychological state of the patient. Addiction to drugs presents itself psychologically, in a manner that is similar to other forms of addiction, such as gambling.

3.   Answer: A. Biomarkers

Explanation: Biomarkers are the best indicators of substance use. Biomarkers will allow you to track a patient's recovery process and identify risks of addiction based upon previous psychological patterns and behaviors. Biomarkers can be detected in both urine and blood tests. These can be used to detect if the patient is using on occasion or if heavy use is present.

4.   Answer: D. Sense of accomplishment

Explanation: There are three different elements contained within the psychological aspect of addiction. With a sense of powerlessness, addiction is often accompanied by feelings of helplessness and powerlessness. The feeling is often experienced after the use of the substance. With a sense of rage, there is an angry feeling that people experience when they suffer emotional injury, and acts as fuel for substance abuse. The rage may cause the person to show irrational, destructive behavioral patterns.

5.   Answer: A. Misuse

Explanation: Misuse is using a drug in a manner, or for a reason that differs from how it was prescribed. Misuse is unintentional.

6.   Answer: D. A person's body is used to taking the drug, and they start to experience withdrawal symptoms when the drug is no longer present in their system.

Explanation: Dependence is a state that occurs when abuse has occurred for a prolonged time. The person can become both mentally and physically addicted. Psychological dependence is a strong mental urge to use a drug to experience effects considered to be pleasant (drugs or alcohol used to reach a euphoric state of mind). Cross-dependence is where a person may use another drug form to lessen the withdrawal they are experiencing from their drug of choice. Physical dependence occurs when a person's body is used to taking the drug, and they start to experience withdraw symptoms when the drug is no longer present in their system.

7.   Answer: B. Half-life

Explanation: The half-life is the amount of time the drug stays present within the body. This level can be affected based upon metabolism and other factors, which differ from the specific half-life of the drug.

8.   Answer: D. All of the above

Explanation: A drug interaction is the way that drugs interact with one another. This includes interactions between street drugs, prescription drugs, and alcohol.

9.   Answer: C. Abuse

Explanation: Abuse is using a drug in a manner other than that prescribed, with the intention of getting high, such as taking too much of one drug within a short period of time.

10.   Answer: D. Reverse tolerance

Explanation: Reverse tolerance can cause a person to become more sensitive to the drug over a period of time, rather than less sensitive. It will cause the substance to have a higher level of impact on the person when taken.

11.   Answer: B. Intravenous

Explanation: The way the drug is administered can affect its method of action. A drug will be stronger when taken intravenously, compared to the oral, injection, or intranasal administration methods.

12.   Answer: C. Both A and B

Explanation: Snorting is commonly used among those who abuse oral medications. While the effects are fast acting, the side-effects can be very dangerous, and in some cases, deadly. Those who use this method of administration can cause severe damage to occur within the sinus cavity, and brain damage can also occur with both short and prolonged usage.

13.   Answer: B. Too much of the medication will be provided during one period of time.

Explanation: Some medications that are taken orally have restrictions that make it necessary for the medication to be taken orally. A time-released medication will need to be taken by mouth and cannot be crushed, or the time release action will be disrupted.

14.   Answer: A. The mucus membranes in the rectum area can absorb some drugs quickly.

Explanation: While not all drugs can be taken rectally, certain drugs such as cocaine can be taken through a suppository. The mucus membranes in the rectum area can absorb some drugs quickly. This method is used by those looking to receive the drug quickly, but this can be risky.

15.   Answer: D. Subcutaneous

Explanation: Subcutaneous injections are done by injecting the drug of choice into the soft tissue present under the skin.

16.   Answer: D. All of the above

Explanation: Drinking is common with alcohol, but certain drugs need to be eaten in order for them to work properly. For example, the illegal street drug LSD requires you to eat the drug in order for it to work, as do "magic mushrooms."

17.   Answer: D. All of the above

Explanation: The risk of an infection is also high when using the injection method, as many drugs require the use of cotton while they are prepared, and this can lead to the cotton getting stuck within the syringe, and being placed under the skin. Infections can also occur due to lack of proper preparation, which creates an unsterile environment when the needle is injected into the skin.

18.   Answer: D. Within five days of the drug use

Explanation: Urine testing must be done within five days of drug use, as the drug begins to leave the urine at this time and an accurate test cannot be conducted.

19.   Answer: A. Blood testing

Explanation: To perform blood testing, a blood sample is taken from the patient with a syringe. This method of testing is one of the most effective for drugs, as drugs can be detected in the blood much faster than urine and saliva, and they also stay in the blood for longer periods of time.

20.   Answer: B. Saliva testing

Explanation: With saliva testing, a swab made from cotton material is used to take a sample of the saliva that is found in the mouth. The mucus membranes within the mouth will have traces of the drug, which will then move into the saliva. This testing is done by using the swab on the inside of the cheek, and then enclosing the swab in a sterilized container that will be sent to a lab for testing.

21.   Answer: D. Up to thirty

Explanation: Drug testing in any of these forms can be done to check for one specific drug, or to check for up to thirty drugs at one time.

22.   Answer: B. The reason for testing

Explanation: The drug testing method used depends upon why it is being done. For example, if the test is taken for legal purposes, the examiner will look for a variety of drugs. However, when being used to help with addiction, one specific drug or those in a similar class are the focus.

23.   Answer: D. Having depression due to alcohol or substance use.

Explanation: Two people using the same substance can have completely different reactions. Addiction is present when the individual has impairment due to the use of the substance. Impairment causes inability to keep a job or attend school, use of substances in high risk situations, such as while driving, legal consequences due to use of drugs, and encountering conflicts due to alcohol of substance use.

24.   Answer: A. Tolerance

Explanation: The biological concept of addiction is based upon genetic factors that influence addiction. Genetics, biochemistry, and metabolism all play a role in addiction factors. Similar to the reaction that some people have to certain foods, some people may be unable to tolerate alcohol, even in small amounts.

25.   Answer: B. MYOB

Explanation: When addiction occurs based on genetic factors, signs of addiction often show before the substance is used. The enzyme MYOB may be lower in the brain of those who are susceptible to alcohol abuse due to their genetic disposition.

26.   Answer: D. fifty percent of the time

Explanation: According to research studies, people with severe mental illnesses only experience success with recovery one-half of the time.

27. **Answer: D. Involving the patient's family**

Explanation: The addiction advocacy movement was created in order to provide recovery to patients by involving their families in order to create a more personalized approach. When connection with families is used as part of a treatment program, long-term recovery is achievable, as this type of plan allows the patients to receive support from their family members while undergoing the recovery process.

28. **Answer: A. A plan that works by implementing a treatment program that provides transformational change in those who are going through the process of recovery.**

Explanation: As patient knowledge continues to expand, the methods used to treat addiction also expand and various techniques used together can provide recovery to patients in a treatment program.

29. **Answer: All of the above**

Explanation: Primary prevention is used for young people or those with little to no history of drug/alcohol abuse.

30. **Answer: C. Decreasing the age of usage, such as age limit to buy alcohol.**

Explanation: Choices A, B, and D are all primary prevention measures, as are increasing the age of usage and promoting safe alternatives by offering community activities to the younger generation.

31. **Answer: B. Prevention**

Explanation: Preventive methods include reducing the available supply of drugs and alcohol through appropriate measures, including legal assistance, reducing the amount of demand present for drugs and alcohol by providing those in the community with appropriate treatment methods, and continuing development of treatment centers to improve the level of care offered.

32.   Answer: B. Secondary prevention

Explanation: Secondary prevention is used to help addicts stop once early usage is detected by way of the HALT Theory. These measures include use intervention method to stop drug/substance use and abuse, education on the risks, dangers, and other negative factors associated with use and abuse, and skill-building techniques to help the client refrain from further use and abuse.

33.   Answer: C. Tertiary prevention

Explanation: Using a specialized approach to treatment which includes desensitizing users to triggers, such as people, places, things, and actions is a form of tertiary prevention. Tertiary prevention is used when drug or alcohol use and abuse has become progressive, and promotes healing of the mind and body.

34.   Answer: C. Tertiary prevention

Explanation: Creating a solid aftercare program for additional treatment once the initial program is complete is a form of tertiary prevention, as is teaching the 12 step principles to the patient in order to prepare him or her once treatment is complete.

35.   Answer: A. Intervention

Explanation: Intervention is a process in which a group of people work together in order to interrupt addiction. This offers addicts several options to stop the process of addiction. Intervention can prevent the individual from hitting rock bottom, and it works to reorient those who have lost touch with reality.

36.   Answer: B. Heavy and non-problematic user

Explanation: A non-user is a person who has not used substances. A moderate or non-problematic user is a person who uses some substances occasionally, but the use has not had a negative effect so far. A heavy and non-problematic user is a person who uses substances heavily, but hasn't seen negative effects. Heavy with serious problems is a person who uses substances very often, and has had many negative events occur. Heavy with moderate problems is a person who uses often and has had a few issues occur. Dependent and addicted with life and health problems is a person who is unable to stop drugs due to physical and mental addiction, and the use and abuse of substances has caused issues in the patients personal life, as well as had a negative effect on their health.

37. Answer: C. Identify, assess, stabilize, rehabilitate

Explanation: Providing treatment for addiction requires the following steps in order for it to be effective: Step 1 - Identify: Screen the areas of the patient's life being effected from the addiction and identify the level of addiction present in the patient. Step 2 - Assess: Collect various pieces of information from the patient, and those involved in the patient's treatment plan identify patient's strengths, weaknesses, and treatment goals. Step 3 - Stabilize: Stop addiction to the substances using appropriate methods. Step 4 - Rehabilitate: Determine the proper long-term treatment program for the patient based upon their individual issues.

38. Answer: B. Aftercare program

Explanation: Co-occurring treatment centers offer treatment to patients who have mental health and substance abuse issues. Inpatient facilities are designed to treat patients who stay at the facility over the course of treatment. Outpatient facilities allow the patient to leave the facility and go home after the treatment is completed each day. Aftercare program are used for patients that have successfully completed an inpatient or outpatient rehab program.

39. Answer: A. Al-Anon

Explanation: Alcoholics Anonymous (AA) is a fellowship of men and women who come together in order to share their experiences, strength and hope for recovery. The only requirement to join this is to have the desire to stop drinking. Narcotics Anonymous (NA) is a non-profit organization meant for men and women who face major drug problems. The meetings are held in order to help maintain sobriety. Al-Teen is a fellowship for younger family members that work off of the same principles as Al-Anon.

40. Answer: D. All of the above

Explanation: HIV is a virus that is contagious and can be spread from one person to another via blood and body fluids. This is a growing epidemic among IV drug users.

Studies show that the HIV has the fastest transition rate among all other sexually transmitted diseases (STDs). It is most common among those who use drugs in the form of administering them with syringe for injection. Early cases of HIV often occur when sexual contact involves the use of drugs.

41.   Answer: D. Sharing hairbrushes

Explanation: During intercourse, the HIV virus is transmitted between people through the mucous membranes in the rectum and vagina. When blood is caught within the needle and injected directly into the non-infected user's vein, this will almost always cause an HIV infection.

42.   Answer: C. She recognizes that substance use is likely to recur.

Explanation: A recovering addict will show readiness for vocational rehabilitation when he or she: recognizes abuse and involvement in the treatment program, shows commitment to recovery, shows progress towards achievement of goals and areas of employment, shows ongoing sobriety, addresses entry issues as part of a better life goal plan, understands why vocational rehabilitation is needed, addresses entry issues as part of a better life call, understands why vocational rehabilitation is an effective program for maintaining sobriety, and is able to independently complete process keeping a job.

43.   Answer: D. Altruism

Explanation: Creating hope is where the counselor offers information and encouragement that things will get better. With bonding, the counselor offers connection that allows the patient to realize they are not alone. Education gives the patient an opportunity to learn about illness, symptoms, and behaviors from group members. Altruism is where the counselor assists the patient to learn they have much to offer in terms of helping others, as this will boost self-esteem.

44.   Answer: A. Discuss events and feelings as the main focus of the group.

Explanation: The counselor must work to encourage expression of group members' emotions in a positive manner.

45.   **Answer: B. Initiate an intervention**

Explanation: The immediate crisis intervention steps are: 1) initiate the intervention; 2) offer hope to the patient with positive statements; 3) provide support to the recovering addict; 4) provide a solution to problem immediately; and 5) give feedback to the patient in a positive manner.

46.   **Answer: C. Empathy**

Explanation: To offer empathy, the counselor must put himself in the patient's shoes in order to develop a true understanding of addiction and related problems.

47.   **Answer: C. Use open-ended questions**

Explanation: Leave questions open-ended in order to encourage the patient to explain things in further detail and develop a deeper understanding.

48.   **Answer: A. Cognitive therapy**

Explanation: Cognitive therapy addresses patterns of thinking and behavior, and methods of handling issues throughout the recovery process. Talk therapy creates a secure and effective environment where the patient can discuss his or her issues in confidence, and the therapist can offer encouragement, support, and positive coping techniques. Hypnosis/EMDR approaches are designed to change the patient's subconscious mind though special techniques, which allow that area of the mind to be accessed. Some professionals feel these two methods can offer lasting change, because they can help the patient deal with issues they were not aware existed.

49.   **Answer: C. Structured analysis**

Explanation: With education, resources are provided to the patient and family members. The recovering addict can utilize outside resources in order to continue on a successful recovery path. Joining involves the ability to connect, understand, and build strength within the families. This helps the recovering addict see how his or her recovery and behavior change can impact the family and how these things interact with one another.

50. **Answer: C. Battering is done because the perpetrator suffers from low self-esteem.**

Explanation: Abusers know it is wrong, and batter in order to feel better about themselves. Abuse is a learned behavior, and many times, the abuser will have suffered abuse in the past. This person uses force to gain control.

51. **Answer: A. Funneling**

Explanation: This is done during individual or couple sessions in order to get information on all aspects involving the abuse, which is generally provided over time in small pieces.

52. **Answer: C. Stage 3**

Explanation: Stage 1: Increased tension is where there is an increase in the amount of tension that occurs within the household. Stage 2: Violence is when the domestic violence occurs. Stage 3: The compensation is where the abuser may become apologetic. Once forgiven, or forgotten, it will almost always start back at stage one. It's important to teach the victim this cycle and how to watch for increased tension again.

53. **Answer: A. Abstinence violation effect (AVE)**

Explanation: AVE describes the circumstances in which an individual engages in a negative behavior like substance abuse after attempting to abstain from it; following the behavior, the individual experiences conflict and/or shame and may use again.

54. **Answer: C. A complete lack of spirituality**

Explanation: The most common issue seen with addiction is a complete lack of spirituality in the patient. Many times, when addiction has become prolonged, negative, and life changing, the patient can experience a disconnection from themselves and from their prior spiritual beliefs.

55. **Answer: All of the above**

Explanation: All of these things should be involved when providing addiction treatment. The counselor cannot push spirituality in order to encourage it within the patient. However, during the initial assessment of the patient, and in order to determine what the patient's feelings toward spirituality are, the counselor should assess this aspect of recovery.

56. **Answer: B. The patient will continue to have doubts throughout the entire recovery process.**

Explanation: Change is observed when the patient makes a connection between his or her life problems and the process of addiction, develops an action plan, takes part in interconnected change and self-discovery, develops a positive self-attitude and maintains it during and after the recovery, maintains hope by using positive coping skills and continues to keep perspective, even during difficult times.

57. **Answer: B. Stage 2 - Preparation**

Explanation: During stage 2 - Preparation, the patient plans to make a change, but may have failed recently or in the past. The patient may have created an incomplete plan and actively participated in it. In this stage, the patient makes small, insignificant changes.

58. **Answer: D. Stage 5 - Termination**

Explanation: Stage 5 - Termination: During the fifth stage, major changes are made. Relaxation is no longer an issue for the patient, as he or she continues to be active in recovery. Although termination can be achieved with the right mind frame, complete termination is often seen as difficult to reach, because addiction is considered to be a life-long, ongoing process of change that needs to be maintained at all times.

59. **Answer: A. 3**

Explanation: The phases are 1) empathy, 2) discrepancy, and 3) resistance.

60.   Answer: B. Discrepancy

Explanation: During phase 2 - discrepancy, the phase is often paired with self-sufficient and empathetic processes. It helps the patient to determine what areas and emotional well-being need to be addressed. The counselor will work with the patient in order to help him or her to develop love and trust in the self.

61.   Answer: B. Dual diagnosis

Explanation: By implementing the proper treatment plan for co-occurring mental disorders, the process of recovery will be much easier for the individual and increase their chance for success.

62.   Answer: A. Gentle approach

Explanation: The gentle approach is a less forceful approach to recovery, which may offer better results for some patients. The multiple intervention approach uses multiple intervention techniques when the patient is reluctant to accept their mental disorder. The unique approach is used when substance abuse and a mental disorder are both present, and a unique treatment plan must be used for the patient.

63.   Answer: A. Assertive Community Therapy Model

Explanation: Assertive community therapy provides a wide range of therapy services. The assertive community therapy model has seven areas of emphasis and creates a natural setting for client care.

64.   Answer: D. Detecting various patient success strategies.

Explanation: The Primary Treatment Assessment Process focuses on addiction treatment and identification of various patient needs for common services. This is done during the assessment process and involves detecting special skills or defects en within the patient, providing basic supplemental needs, identifying the level of regular ability to function, and detecting various patient risk strategies.

65.   Answer: B. Moral decisions

Explanation: Moral decisions are decisions made by a counselor in a manner that regards the patient's best interest. The decision that is made involves policy, the right attitude, and appropriate behaviors on a case-by-case basis.

66.   Answer: C. Ethical principles

Explanation: Ethical principles create moral decisions involving patient care and value. Aspects of ethical practice include moral decisions, laws, and principles.

67.   Answer: B. A disclosure of records

Explanation: In order for the information to be provided to the medical professional, there must be a prior authorization provided by the patient. Authorization is made when the patient signs a disclosure of records, which is done in the presence of the counselor who is providing the treatment to the patient. With the area of confidentiality regarding ethics, a judgment of overall privilege for proper administration of justice allows information given under certain exceptions.

68.   Answer: A. Duty to warn

Explanation: Duty to warn is a process where the counselor providing treatment to the patient needs to determine whether serious danger is present. To assess the situation, the counselor should first talk to the supervisor in charge of the treatment plan to obtain assistance in making the correct decision. After this, the case should be referred to the police, so the potential victim can receive the care that he or she needs in order to reduce serious harm.

69.   Answer: D. All of the above

Explanation: Gender, method of administration, and strength of the drug all determine the level of addiction present.

70.   Answer: C. A medicine

Explanation: A drug is an illegal substance used to create a high within the body. A medicine is a substance prescribed to a patient to treat a condition. It may have a potential for abuse, and if this is present, the use of the drug should be monitored.

71.   Answer: B. Dependence

Explanation: Dependence is a state that occurs when drug or alcohol abuse has occurred for a prolonged period of time. The person can become both mentally and physically addicted to the drug. Misuse is using a drug in a manner, or for a reason, that differs from how it was prescribed. This type of use is unintentional. Psychological dependence occurs when a person has a strong mental urge to use a drug to experience the effects considered to be pleasant (drug or alcohol used to reach a euphoric state of mind).

72.   Answer: C. Cross-dependence

Explanation: With cross-dependence, a person may use another drug form to lessen the withdrawal they are experiencing from their drug of choice. Abuse is using a drug in a manner other than that prescribed, with the intention of getting high, such as taking too much of one drug within a short period of time.

73.   Answer: B. Reverse tolerance

Explanation: Reverse tolerance will cause a substance to have a higher level of impact on a person when taken.

74.   Answer: C. The therapeutic dose

Explanation: The therapeutic dose is the amount of drug needed by the person in order for it to be effective.

75.   Answer: D. All of the above

Explanation: When drugs are taken through injections, there are additional risks that are present. While the risk of overdose is high with this method of administration, the risk of contracting a disease is also increased greatly. This is because if a needle is shared, disease can be easily spread.

76.   Answer: A. "Shrooms"

Explanation: "Shrooms" or "magic mushrooms" contain a psychedelic/euphoric substance called psilocybin.

77.   Answer: C. Provide more accurate results

Explanation: If the test needs additional screening, it can be sent to a laboratory, which will provide more accurate testing results. This includes the amount of the drug present in the urine, which can indicate the amount being used and the last time the drug was used.

78.   Answer: C. A swab made from cotton material is used to take a sample of the saliva on the inside of the cheek, and then the swab is enclosed in a sterilized container that will be sent to a lab for testing.

Explanation: The mucus membranes within the mouth will have traces of the drug, which will then move into the saliva. This testing is done by using the swab on the inside of the cheek, and then enclosing the swab in a sterilized container that will be sent to a lab for testing.

79.   Answer: A. 1

Explanation: One blood sample is all that is needed, regardless of the amount of drugs being assessed.

80.   Answer: A. Impairment due to substance use

Explanation: Impairment causes the inability to keep a job or attend school, use of substances in high risk situations, such as while driving, legal consequences due to the use of drugs, and encountering conflicts due to alcohol or substance use.

81.   Answer: D. A 132-pound woman

Explanation: Similar to the reaction that some people have to certain foods, some people may be unable to tolerate alcohol, even when consumed in small amounts. Their bodies will act adversely to the substance, and behavioral issues will occur. Women tend to have a lower tolerance to alcohol then men.

82.   Answer: A. Bubbly personality

Explanation: When addiction occurs based on genetic factors, signs of addiction often show before the substance is used. Signs are seen at a young age, which include violent behaviors, impulsive behaviors, and lacking social skills.

83.   Answer: D. Cultural therapy

Explanation: The counselor should provide several levels of patient care to the patient, and individual, group, and family therapy should be used in conjunction when appropriate.

84.   Answer: A. Transformational change

Explanation: The concept of recovery in addiction is a plan that works by implementing a treatment program that provides transformational change in those who are going through the process of recovery. As knowledge continues to expand, the methods used to treat addiction also expand and various techniques used together can provide recovery to patients.

85.   Answer: B. The patient's mental health issue is treated.

Explanation: By treating the patient's mental health issue, the chance of a successful recovery is increased. Therapy is used to help the patient gain the skills needed for long-term recovery.

86.   Answer: A. A prevention group

Explanation: Prevention groups are defined as a group of individuals who are working together in order to provide education on drug use to a target group. The groups included in the process of intervention include the general population, at-risk individuals, and high-risk individuals.

87. Answer: C. To stop drug use from occurring.

Explanation: The main goal of a prevention group is to stop drug use from occurring, but also to address the issue of abuse if it should occur by catching it while in the early stages.

88. Answer: B. Prevention

Explanation: Preventive methods include reducing the available supply of drugs and alcohol through appropriate measures, including legal assistance, reducing the amount of demand present for drugs and alcohol by providing those in the community with appropriate treatment methods, and continuing development of treatment centers to improve the level of care offered.

89. Answer: A. Primary prevention

Explanation: Primary prevention is used for young people or those with little to no history of drug/alcohol abuse. It is applied by promoting abstinence from drugs and alcohol, teaching refusal skills to those who haven't used it, increasing usage policies, such as the age limit to buy alcohol, providing education on the dangers associated with drugs and alcohol use, and promoting safe alternatives by offering community activities to younger people.

90. Answer: B. Assisting a patient with using support services and available resources.

Explanation: If a patient requires addiction support that does not fall within the scope of your facility, you may need to refer him or her. A referral involves assisting the patient to use support services and available resources.

91. Answer: A. Getting all the pertinent information possible

Explanation: During a crisis interview, it is important to gather all pertinent information that you possibly can. This will allow you to make decisions regarding the patient's care and determine what needs to be done.

92.   Answer: B. Contact child protective services to report this.

Explanation: Because the mother left the children alone, they are at risk for harm and neglect has occurred. The proper authorities should be notified, as the children may need medical care and other services.

93.   Answer: D. "Your story is quite confusing."

Explanation: To let the patient know that you are aware of the discrepancies, the counselor should inform him of this.

94.   Answer: A. Using pharmaceutical approaches.

Explanation: Tertiary prevention is used when drug or alcohol use and abuse has become progressive. The counselor must apply intervention processes to stop drug use and encourage recovery, send the patient to an appropriate detoxification (detox) facility, use recovery treatment centers after detox is complete, use a specialized approach to treatment which includes desensitizing users to triggers, and using pharmaceutical approaches to help the recovery process.

95.   Answer: B. Detached caring

Explanation: The intervention process involves meeting with the family and significant others of the addict, who will be assisted through the process with the help of a counselor. The process is successful when applied using the correct measures of detached caring.

96.   Answer: D. All of the above

Explanation: While an intervention is not always successful for the addict, the process can still be successful for those involved. This is because it offers different benefits, which include coming together for the first time as a family since the addiction, started, learning techniques that each family member can use for their own self-help process, stopping denial of the addiction in both family members and the addict, and learning as a group how to stop enabling addiction.

97.   Answer: C. Heavy user with moderate problems

Explanation: A non-user is a person that does not or has not used substances. A moderate and non-problematic user uses some substances occasionally, but the use has not had a negative effect on the patient's life so far. A heavy and non-problematic user uses substances heavily, but hasn't had negative effects occur in health or life. A heavy with serious problems uses substances very often, and has had many negative events occur due to use. A heavy with moderate problems uses often and has had a few issues occur as a result of the use.

98.   Answer: C. Dependent and addicted with life and health problems

Explanation: Dependent and addicted with life and health problems describes a person who is unable to stop drugs due to physical and mental addiction, and who has issues in their personal life, as well as negative effects on their health.

99.   Answer: C. Step 3 - Stabilize

Explanation: During the third step (stabilization), the counselor helps the addict stop addiction to the substance using appropriate methods. Some methods include detox and use of pharmaceutical alternatives in order to help stop mental addiction to drugs, and creating a secure recovery foundation.

100.   Answer: D. Step 4 - Rehabilitate

Explanation: To rehabilitate the addict, the counselor determines the proper long-term treatment program for the patient based upon the issues detected during the assessment and development of overall treatment plan.

101.   Answer: D. Outpatient treatment centers

Explanation: Inpatient facilities are designed to treat patients who stay at the facility over the entire course of treatment. Treatment generally lasts from one to six months. Outpatient facilities offer the same type of care as inpatient rehabilitation facilities, except the patient leaves the facility and goes home after treatment is completed each day.

102.   Answer: B. Goals are based on the counselor's desires

Explanation: An important part of any treatment program is to set goals with the patient. Goals are based upon the patient's desires, and are created using realistic measures.

103.   Answer: A. Makes is easier for the patient to achieve sobriety

Explanation: Goal setting offers many benefits, but achieving sobriety will never be easy for a patient.

104.   Answer: C. Group Therapy

Group therapy offers the patient the ability to participate in a group setting with peers who also face addiction. Group therapy gives the patient the opportunity to relate to others who are going through similar issues, as well as to develop a support team.

105.   Answer: A. Alcoholics Anonymous

Explanation: Many self-help groups use the Twelve Steps, which were created as the original principles for Alcoholics Anonymous.

106.   Answer: C. Is open to addicts regardless of their drug of choice (including alcohol).

Explanation: Narcotics Anonymous is a 12-step program similar to Alcoholics Anonymous; however, its literature and meetings focus on addiction rather than any one specific drug.

107.   Answer: A. Working with other people in recovery.

Explanation: An addict in recovery should guide another addict through the Twelve Steps.

108.   Answer: D. All of the above.

Explanation: Self-help Twelve Step programs like AA and NA describe themselves as fellowships, or peer groups, of people who come together to help each other achieve sobriety and recovery through working the Twelve Steps and following the principles behind them.

109.   Answer: A. Occupational Safety and Health Administration (OSHA)

Explanation: All addicts should be considered to be infected with HIV, whether test results confirm this or not. The universal guidelines fall under the national Institute of Occupational Safety and Health Administration (OSHA).

110.   Answer: D. Blood and body fluids

Explanation: HIV is a virus that is contagious and can be spread from one person to another via blood and body fluids. HIV is a growing epidemic among IV drug users.

111.   Answer: C. Human Immunodeficiency Virus (HIV)

Explanation: Studies show that the HIV has the fastest transition rate among all other sexually transmitted diseases (STDs).

112.   Answer: B. When members engage in unprotected sexual activity with multiple other members of the group

Explanation: If members of a group have regular unprotected sex with multiple members, they risk transmitting HIV and other STDs.

113.   Answer: A. It will die.

Explanation: The HIV virus lives within cells and dies once it is outside of the body.

114.   Answer: C. The person has a suppressed immune system.

Explanation: Once the HIV virus is passed to another individual, it spreads rapidly. It is most powerful during the days and weeks immediately following infection.

115. Answer: B. HIV can be suppressed for many years, and HIV positive people can live normal, healthy lives.

Explanation: Treatment can be provided for HIV. While there is no cure for this disease, medication can suppress it for several years and delay its progression to AIDS. However, it can still be transmitted.

116. Answer: D. Hearing loss

Explanation: Early symptoms of HIV include flu-like symptoms, changes in vision, fatigue, and unexplained fevers.

117. Answer: A. Sex is often offered in exchange for drugs when addiction has progressed.

Explanation: As HIV and other STDs are more prevalent among other drug users, when addicts turn to offering sex in exchange for drugs, they put themselves at greater risk of contracting an infection.

118. Answer: B. Stop the spread of STDs.

Explanation: The process of risk reduction counseling involves using substance-abuse prevention in order to stop the spread of STDs. This form of counseling offers information regarding transmission and risky behaviors.

119. Answer: All of the above

Explanation: When the addict is actively using drugs, the counselor can provide proper coping skills, give information on additional changes designed to build the immune system, discuss the benefits of exercise, teach self-exams to detect issues regarding health, and provide the patient with information on the steps he or she can take for a rapid and healthy lifestyle change.

120. Answer: D. Personal friendships

Explanation: External resources include housesitting, a residential program, home healthcare, support groups, and info and treatment options that are available. While a friendly professional relationship can be beneficial, personal friendships outside of treatment go beyond the professional boundaries of counselor-client relationships.

121. Answer: D. Relapse

Explanation: The counselor should discuss different treatment options that are available for the patient regarding the disease. While treatment must be focused upon recovery from substance abuse, it should also be used to discuss the virus or other STD in a manner that gives hope to the patient.

122. Answer: C. Both recovery from drug and alcohol use and prevention of STDs

Explanation: Pre-infection advice includes proper education on the different types of STDs, how they affect a person's life, instruction on the use of standard precautions as a part of everyday life, aiming treatment towards both recovery from drugs and alcohol and prevention of STDs and taking steps to identify and stop relapse.

123. Answer: D. Train alongside experienced mentors

Explanation: In some cases, counselors train alongside experienced mentors and work to apply the mental text to settings in order to gain experience.

124. Answer: C. Bonding

Explanation: The therapeutic techniques the counselor offers to patients must help them stay in recovery by creating hope.

125. Answer: D. Developing social skills

Explanation: Resolving conflicts involves taking steps to resolve any conflicts with the people who reconnect by sitting in and offering positive monitoring. Initiating lost connections is where the counselor encourages members of group to reconnect with important people in their life who were lost due to the addiction, such as close friends and family members. Copying actions is where members will see positive behaviors among some other group members and want to copy and mimic these behaviors. Developing social skills is where the counselor helps a member to listen and take part in different group activities in order to improve or reconnect with their social skills, such as taking part in role playing activities.

126.   Answer: A. Subconscious feelings

Explanation: With subconscious feelings, group members will have deep fears and hidden feelings arise during the discussions, which will allow these issues to be addressed and worked through.

127.   Answer: B. Develop appropriate confrontational techniques

Explanation: Developing appropriate confrontational techniques allows recovering addicts to learn how to express negative feelings to others in a positive manner.

128.   Answer: A. By expressing emotions and seeing the same emotions within group members, the recovering addict will begin to recognize negative behavior patterns in his or her life and develop a plan to change them

Explanation: Connecting with other positive members and the counselor will allow the recovering addict to develop a strong support group that can aid them through their recovery.

129.   Answer: C. Offer support to the patient's family

Explanation: The counselor should implement actions for crisis intervention and resolution, such as helping to create a resolution with the patient, securing a safe environment for the patient and other group members, determining the cause of the crisis, offering support and additional resources to the family and helping the patient create a plan for action.

130.   Answer: B. Individual counseling

Explanation: Individual counseling offers the patients the ability to work on a one-on-one basis with counselor. This form of treatment can offer the recovering addict the ability to express deep issues and concerns that he or she may not feel comfortable with expressing within a group setting.

131.   Answer: C. The recovering addict will have a better chance at recovery.

Explanation: The counselor can provide the patient with a sense of security during the individual counseling, which will create an environment that is secure enough for the patient to acknowledge and address issues they may be afraid to confront. If individual counseling is used along with group therapy, the recovering addict has a greater chance of recovery.

132.   Answer: B. Paraphrasing

Explanation: Paraphrasing gives the patient the ability to hear their own words – stated slightly differently - and evaluate them critically.

133.   Answer: A. Offering simplicity

Explanation: To offer simplicity, the counselor will take complex issues the patient is facing and offer simple solutions that can be used to resolve the conflict.

134.   Answer: C. Talk therapy

Explanation: This form of therapy encourages the patient to express his or her feelings.

135.   Answer: C. Both A and B

Explanation: Individual counseling may be short- or long-term, based upon the patient's particular case.

136.   Answer: D. All of the above

Explanation: The recovering addict's family plays an important role in both the active addiction and recovery process. According to addiction experts, these people may take part in the use, abuse, or overuse of substances and enable the patient to further use drugs or alcohol.

137.   Answer: A. Coping techniques

Explanation: The counselor working with family members can work to create change within the family structure, create techniques within the family that can help to reach a higher level of function, provide strength to the members of the family, and offer different coping techniques to family members during the therapy session.

138.   Answer: C. Structured analysis

Explanation: The recovering addict can utilize outside resources in order to continue on a successful recovery path. Alternative coping techniques are when the counselor teaches honest demonstration of feelings to family members so that they can express their emotions and determine how they can use them to solve issues.

139.   Answer: B. Drug substitution

Explanation: Drug substitution is the substitution of a legal drug for an illegal one to assist the patient in making positive life changes.

140.   Answer: C. Use drugs to cope with the abuse.

Explanation: Many women who are subjected to abuse seek partners who have problems with addiction. Counselors must determine the dynamics that surround the use and abuse.

141.   Answer: C. Eliminating blame

Explanation: Eliminating blame helps the patient to realize they are responsible for the abuse, not the substance.

142.   Answer: C. Enhanced self-worth

Explanation: Issues often seen with children who are part of a household involving addiction include lack of trust, no sense of self-worth, boundary issues, lack of feelings, impulsivity, self-harm, and other negative feelings projected on themselves or onto others.

143.   Answer: B. That he or she is not responsible for the addiction

Explanation: The counselor should determine how both the adolescent and the user may play a role within that addiction process. It is important to tell the adolescent that he or she is not responsible for the addiction but that anyone can accidentally be an enabler.

144.   Answer: D. Long-term negative effects for the entire family

Explanation: A continued denial of the addiction will lead to long-term negative effects for the entire family, and this could result in death due to overdose, brought on by the family's unintentional enabling.

145.   Answer: D. All of the above

Explanation: Assessment is the collection of data from the individual and corroborative sources to determine the extent of the individual's problem and their strengths, weaknesses, and needs. This information is used to formulate the plan of treatment to include goals, methods and resources.

146.   Answer: D. Individualized

Explanation: Substance abuse and associated treatment services should be individualized and appropriate to the needs of the patient.

147.   Answer: B. A case manager

Explanation: Case management should be used to ensure that patients receive all necessary services in a timely and coordinated manner. The utilization of individual, group, and family/significant other counseling should be utilized as needed to assist in meeting the needs of the patient.

148.   Answer: A. Ongoing processes

Explanation: Recovery and relapse are both ongoing processes, not an event. Thus, relapse prevention should be approached as a process with the identification of individualized triggers and a plan to confront those triggers should they occur.

Relapse prevention should be made a valuable part of the client's aftercare program and discharge goals.

149.   Answer: A. What happens when a person fails to abstain from a negative habitual behavior

Explanation: AVE relates to what happens when a person fails to abstain from a negative habitual behavior, such as drug use, and then faces conflict and guilt.

150.   Answer: A. Psychological and behavioral issues involved in the addiction process

Explanation: The Professional Experience Questionnaire is a 40-question test that examines psychological and behavioral issues involved in the addiction process.

Made in the USA
Middletown, DE
13 February 2019